HEROES FOR ALL TIME

Stories of inspiring heroism from Russian history

NICHOLAS KOTAR

WAYSTONE
PRESS

FOREWORD

We stand on the shoulders of giants. Shame on us that we don't know more about them. As a child of immigrants, I was raised on stories of a glorious Holy Russia that I knew better than the San Francisco of my childhood. That land was filled with heroes who gave their lives for God, Tsar, and country and who left legacies that all of us children aspired to.

Of course, so much of that was legend, a lifeline for immigrants who had lost everything, and who preferred to remember a semi-fictional history that left out some of the more disturbing details.

As I grew up and learned the more nuanced truth, I only became more fascinated. Because what I found was this: despite the almost universal darkness of the human condition, you still have bright lights appearing in unexpected places—heroes and heroines whose lives read like adventure tales, whose fates are sometimes stranger than fiction.

As a writer of speculative fiction, I find inspiration in these stories and often mine them for my novels and short stories. Over the past few years, all the research I've done for my *Raven*

Son series has turned up a wealth of fascinating accounts from Russian history that make for interesting reading all on its own.

This little book is a glimpse into the world of my Russia— a world filled with complex characters living out difficult lives in sometimes impossible circumstances. But more often then not, they rose above these difficulties to become truly heroic. In our own chaotic time, their stories are worthy of being retold again and again.

THE PRINCE WHO WAS KILLED
BY HIS FAVORITE HORSE

The early years of ancient Russia's history are so steeped in legend that it's perhaps more correct to categorize them as "strange as fiction" not "stranger than fiction." But there are good reasons for that.

The boundary between history and legend used to be malleable. People were not always so in love with facts as we moderns seem to be. And, frankly, that made historical accounts and chronicles a lot more interesting to read. Who cares if some of what we read is legendary? That's not a bad word in my book.

One of the most famous examples of such a half-legendary, half-historical hero from old Rus is Prince Oleg the Seer.

OLEG: THE PRINCE WHO WAS KILLED BY HIS FAVORITE HORSE

Prince Oleg the Seer is one of the most mysterious figures in early Russian history. He was either related to Riurik, the half-mythical Varengian who unified Rus, or his main general. But he did much more than Riurik to unify Rus. While Riurik's son Igor was still a child, Oleg seized Smolensk and Liubech, both important cities. He also tricked and killed the princes of Kiev, Askold and Dir, and made their city the cultural and political center of Rus under his control.

All the disparate tribes of Slavs eventually came to accept his sovereignty as "Grand Prince" of Rus.

He also had major successes in foreign affairs. For two hundred years before Oleg, the Khaganate of the Khazars had successfully demanded tribute from the Eastern Slavic lands. Oleg was the first to fight them openly, and he was almost always successful. He even managed to make Byzantium sit up and take notice. During his reign, Russian merchants received the right—unique for the time—of duty-free trade with Constantinople. The Greeks also gave the Russians nearly unlimited materials and artisans to repair their boats. For free!

For these reasons, some historian prefer to consider Oleg, not Riurik, as the true unifier of Rus. However, if that list of achievements sounds too good to be true, it might be.

THE INVASION THAT NEVER WAS

Oleg is popularly most known for attacking Constantinople, after which he received his nickname "the Seer." According to the Chronicles, the Prince gathered two thousand ships, each one of which was able to carry forty warriors. The emperor at the time, Leo VI "the Philosopher," was so afraid at the mere sight of such army that he closed the inner gates of the city, leaving the outskirts of his empire open to looting.

However, instead of attacking, Oleg chose trickery. As the Chronicle says,

 He ordered his men to make wheels and to place his ships on those wheels. And when a favorable wind blew, they raised sails and sailed to the city on dry land.

After this, the Greeks, scared to death, offered Oleg tribute

and peace. According to this peace treaty of 907, Russian merchants received the right to duty-free trade. However, although basically every Russian medieval source mentions this invasion, most historians believe it to be no more than legend. First of all, no Byzantine source mentions it, even though similar invasions on the part of Slavs were recorded in both 860 and 941. The peace treaty of 907 also raises more questions. It seems to be a compilation of several other treaties, including one from 911, when Oleg apparently sent an embassy to Constantinople to confirm the peace.

More than that, the exact description of the Russians' return with booty sounds like it was copied from previous accounts. For one, their sails were supposed to have been made from gold silk, a detail that is found in the same Chronicle's account of Prince Vladimir's return from Constantinople after his baptism. A similar description can also be found in a 12th century saga about King Olaf of Norway's return from a successful war:

 It was said that after a certain victory he returned home, and his ships were so magnificent and majestic that their sails were sewed from precious silks, as were their pavilions.

WHAT ABOUT THE SNAKE?

Oleg's other claim to fame comes from a popular folk song that describes an episode, also found in the Chronicle. According to this tale, a pagan priest predicted that Oleg would be killed by his favorite horse. Heartbroken at this prophecy, Oleg ordered that his horse be taken away. He only remembered the prophecy much later, years after his favorite horse had died.

Laughing at the priests, Oleg went to see the place where his horse's bones lay. When he put his foot on the horse's skull, he said, "Is this what I should fear?" At that very moment, a poisonous snake came out of the skull and bit him.

This is clearly a legend—a legendary death for a semi-legendary warrior-prince. This was actually a popular literary trope for sagas of the time. Such deaths gave more importance to the lives of great heroes. Thus, for example, the Icelandic sagas tell of a certain Viking named Örvard-Oddr. According to Wikipedia, "when he was an infant, a druid predicted that he would be killed by his own horse Faxi, at the place where he was born, at the age of 300."

Oddr killed his own horse and threw it into a pit and covered its body with stones. Later, like Oleg, he also visited Faxi's grave and mocked the prophecy. But then:

> When they walked away quickly, Oddr struck his foot and bent down. "What was it that I struck with my foot?" He touched it with the point of his spear, and all saw that it was the skull of a horse. Immediately, a snake slithered out of it and attacked Oddr and bit him in the foot above his ankle. The poison immediately acted, and his leg swelled up all the way to the hip.

To this day, it's actually not clear who copied the story from whom. It's hard to determine the exact date of Oleg's death from the Chronicle, especially since the original manuscript was rewritten many times. All we know for sure is that Örvard-Oddr is a fictional character who was probably invented no earlier than the 13th century. What is possible also is that the tragic death by snakebite is a Scandinavian story trope that made its way into Rus together with the Varengians, finding its final Russian form in the half-legendary traditions surrounding Prince Oleg. However, some historians insist that Örvard-Oddr and Oleg are actually one and the same, and both fictional.

In any case, it makes for a great story.

THE PERSIAN SAGA

It's a well known fact that medieval Russians were enamored of Alexander the Great (see chapter 3). It's possible that Alexander's famous death in the East inspired another, little-known version of Oleg's death. One of the earliest Russian chronicles is the *Novgorodian Chronicle*. It calls Oleg "Igor's voyevoda (i.e. chief military commander)" and mentions that he may have died in a military adventure "beyond the seas."

It's possible that this military adventure is the one described by the Arabian writer Al-Masudi (sometimes called the Herodotus of the Arabs). Al-Masudi describes a fleet of 500 Russian ships that attacked the Kerch Strait in 912, led by two warriors he names as "Al-dir and Olvang." This second leader could, in fact, be Oleg.

The story of this invasion was as follows. The Khan of the Khazars allowed the Rus access through the Don River to the Volga, and from there into the Caspian Sea. In return, he was to receive half of their spoils of war. The goal of this adventure was the legendary riches of Persia itself. One of the results of this invasion was the almost complete destruction of Persian Azerbaijan.

When the loot from "Persia" came back to the Khazars, some of the Khan's Moslem mercenaries were so incensed at the death of their fellow Moslems in Azerbaijan that they decided to attack the Russians. The Khan of the Khazars didn't warn his Russian "allies," and, according to the Novgorod Chronicle, 30,000 Russian were killed in a surprise attack. The rest escaped up the Volga, but were finished off by Bulgarian warriors.

Some historians prefer this version of Oleg's death to the more legendary one. However, being a lover of legends myself, I will always choose the horse-head version.

OLGA: THE VIKING QUEEN OF THE RUS

L ike her male namesake, Olga was a fascinating figure, her life dramatic, cinematic, her story seemingly torn from an adventure novel. Her life's journey, from being the wife of a grand prince to furiously avenging his death to becoming a diplomat with international importance, lends itself wonderfully to the imagination.

However, her life is documented in ways that Oleg's isn't. So, in a way, she was a bridge between the world of the legends and the new historical reality. She also incarnated a cultural shift from paganism to Christianity that would, several generations later, be reflected in the life of her entire nation.

THE WIFE OF IGOR

After the death of the great warrior Oleg, the unstable polity of Kievan Rus began to fall apart. The Drevlians, one of the several Slavic tribes living in the area, rose up against their Varengian overlords, trying to separate from Kiev's control. It didn't help that a new horde of asiatic nomads, the Pechenegs, approached the borders of Rus at the same time. But Igor took care of both problems with a sure hand. He reconquered the Drevlians and laid a heavy tribute on them (Igor became their new and most hated enemy after that). As for the Pechenegs, he managed to use diplomacy, backed with a faithful and powerful army.

Igor's rule saw the continuing unification of the East Slavic tribes. Now all of Rus paid tribute to Kiev directly.

By this time, Igor was married to the Varengian Olga, who was a member of a prominent family (other versions have her as Oleg's daughter). Some stories say that Igor saw her when he was hunting in the forests near Pskov as a young man, and he was captivated by her beauty and her sharp mind.

An interesting historical point about their married life: they were monogamous. This wasn't all that common in early Rus, when princes were allowed many wives. But it was a testament to the strength of their bond and their humaneness in general.

Her Varengian name was Helga, and the Slavicized version (Olga) is a feminized version of "Oleg," which means "holy." Though the pagan understanding of holiness is completely different from the Christian one, it still does assume a special spiritual disposition, chastity and sobriety, intelligence and even prescience. Not surprisingly, the people came to call Oleg a "seer," while they came to call Olga "the Wise."

IGOR'S AVENGING FURY

Igor was killed by treachery in the middle of the day, while gathering tribute from the Drevlians. It seemed that his death would lead to the complete dissolution of Rus, especially since Olga was left as regent in Kiev for her small son, the future Prince Sviatoslav. Immediately, the Drevlians separated from Kiev and refused to pay any more tribute. However, the rest of the Russian elite united around Olga and not only acknowledged her right to rule as regent, but followed her lead without demur.

By that time, Olga was in the prime of her physical and spiritual powers. Legends were told of her beauty and her wit, even in surrounding countries, as far as Byzantium itself.

From the first moments of her rule, Olga showed herself to be confident, authoritative, visionary, even cruel. First of all, she had her revenge against the Drevlians.

The *Chronicles* relate a fascinating and dramatic story. The Drevlians, perhaps realizing how tenuous their position was, decided to entice Olga with an offer of marriage to their own ruler, a man named Mal. This embassy had another meaning as well, clearly understood to any politician of the time. It was an olive branch—Olga was being offered a new husband, and in return she would not avenge the murdered one.

Olga pretended to accept the ambassadors with honors. She invited them to the court on the next day. They were to be carried in boats by her own warriors as a special honor. But instead, she had a ditch dug near her own palace, and when the ambassadors, full of their own importance, were carried in on longboats, she ordered them thrown into the ditch and buried alive.

Immediately after that, Olga required that the Drevlians send another embassy. It was the custom in Rus to offer ambassadors the use of a steam room to wash before official proceedings began. After a long road, the wash was a pleasant thing, and it also carried a hint of ritual ablution. No sooner had these new ambassadors entered the steam room than the doors were locked and the house was set on fire. They were burned alive.

Finally, Olga herself traveled to the land of the Drevlians to celebrate a pagan ritual feast over the grave of her killed husband and to mourn him. When the nobles of the Drevlians had drunk a large amount of alcoholic beverages, Olga ordered all of her warriors, who were sober, to kill them all where they sat, at the foot of the mound where her husband was interred.

Olga, the pagan, had her revenge like a pagan. There was something of the ritual in it. This triple revenge followed the usual pattern for Slavic burial customs. Bodies were typically laid in boats after death—an old Russian tradition. Cremation was also typical for all Russian lands. Sometimes, human sacrifices during the ritual feast over the grave of the dead were practiced as well.

But now, once the ritual vengeance was concluded, Olga began her personal vendetta.

She had her armies attack the main city of the Drevlians, Iskorosten'. In open battle, the Drevlians were routed. The *Chronicle* vividly describes how Sviatoslav, still a boy, began the battle by hurling his small spear in the direction of the enemy. The remainder of their army and the rest of the civilians hid behind the walls of the city. The siege lasted several months. Finally, only guile managed to bring the city down.

Olga seemed to soften in her demands by asking a small tribute—three sparrows and three pigeons from each household. She promised to leave soon afterward. As soon as the tribute was collected, Olga had her warriors tie burning tinder to the feet of the birds. Then they were released. Since all the birds were homing, they returned to their households. Soon the entire city was ablaze, and the Kievan army began their assault.

OLGA THE WISE POLITICIAN

Olga unified the tribes not only with cruelty and guile. As a wise and far-seeing ruler, she realized that the pagan ways of vendetta didn't make for any lasting unity. So she instituted reforms, including a new system of tribute. From now on, the tribute amount couldn't randomly be changed by the ruling authority, and the cities themselves had to bring it to special collecting agencies once a year. From there, the tribute made its way to Kiev.

Then Olga and her armies traveled all through the rest of the cities, instituting this standardized from of tribute and the collection agencies throughout Rus. This was the first organized system of taxation in Rus. According to the *Chronicle*, this led to a flourishing period for the newly-unified Rus.

These collection agencies also served as local courts and as official representatives of the princely power in Kiev. Perhaps not surprisingly, these agencies were organized most often in the centers of cities, where markets were usually held. So these spots, associated with Kiev's power, became the nexuses for ethnic and cultural unity for the Russian tribes.

Later, when Olga became Christian, she built Rus's first churches right next to these government outposts. During Vladimir's time, they even became conflated in the newly-formed unit called the parish. Olga also put a lot of money and effort into improving infrastructure throughout Rus. Of course, any regularly enforced system of taxation takes a little time to become accepted throughout, so Olga made sure to live on one of Kiev's hills, surrounded by a wall and her best warrior band near her at all times.

OLGA THE DIPLOMAT

Having laid the foundation for unity at home, Olga turned to international affairs. She had to show that the time of difficulty following Igor's death did not weaken Rus's international authority. Historians note that during her reign, the first border between Poland and Rus was formed. Massive frontier outposts in the south guarded that part of Rus from invasion by nomadic Asiatic tribes. More and more foreigners came to Rus to trade.

This new influx of money allowed Kiev to start building in stone. Eventually, Kiev became a kind of wonder of the ancient world, known throughout the East and West.

But Olga realized that all this was only window dressing. While the different tribes followed different religious traditions, there was always the threat of disunity. Rus was becoming a major international player, and she thought that a single religion would go a long way to encourage Rus's continued growth, especially with the Eastern Roman Empire and the Saxon kingdoms to contend with.

Olga saw that, culturally speaking, both the Greeks and the

Saxons were far more advanced than the Rus, and she understood that the bedrock of that culture was the Christian religion. She began to be convinced more and more that Rus's future path of greatness lay not only in military exploits, but through spiritual achievements.

Leaving Kiev to Sviatoslav, Olga traveled in 954 with a large fleet bound for Constantinople. This was a peaceful fleet (unlike her father Oleg's famous attack on the Imperial City), which was both diplomatic and religious in nature. However, political expediency demanded a show of military force in the Black Sea, so that the proud Greeks would remember Oleg and not simply brush off his daughter as insignificant.

It had the desired result. Olga was admitted into the Emperor's presence, with Constantine VII Porphyrogenites even organizing a feast in her honor. During their conversations, Olga and the Emperor confirmed the previous treaty struck between Constantinople and Rus in Igor's time.

THE QUESTION OF BAPTISM

At the same time, Olga was dumbfounded by the luxury and grandeur of Constantinople, as well as by its cosmopolitan nature. Many nations spoke different languages in its streets. But more than anything she was astounded by the spiritual richness of Christianity, its churches and the holy objects held in them. She was present at liturgies in all the major churches, including Hagia Sophia. This was what she wanted for her land: this grandeur and this holiness.

One of the major questions discussed with the Emperor ended up being Olga's baptism into the Christian faith.

Most nations of Western Europe had accepted Christianity by this point, either from Rome or Constantinople. These nations, having accepted baptism 300-600 years before the Rus, had out-gained the Rus culturally by a significant margin.

However, paganism held fast in Eastern Europe and wouldn't go down without a fight.

Olga understood that Christianity was necessary if she wanted the cultural riches of the Greeks and the West. Still, she recognized the power of paganism and the strength it held over her people's imaginations. Therefore, she chose a moderate path. She decided to become a Christian alone, hoping by her example to inspire her fellow countrymen.

Finally, it's important to note that for Olga, accepting Christianity was not merely a political decision. It was an answer for many of her internal questions and worries. She had suffered a good amount in her life—the death of a beloved husband, a violent series of acts to avenge his death, burning an entire city of civilians—all this couldn't help but leave its mark on her soul. After all, Olga was always one to strive for rightness. She tried always to be fair and humane to all.

Some of the Chronicles even go so far as to suggest that the Emperor was besotted by her beauty and intelligence, even asking for her hand in marriage. That is highly unlikely—the Greeks, for all their diplomacy, considered the barbarian Rus as little more than talking animals. But it does make for a good story. Ultimately, Olga refused his hand, the story goes, instead asking him to be her godfather.

That part at least seems to have been historically possible. She was given the name Helen after the mother of Constantine the Great. Constantine VII's wife was also name Helen. This moment, with Olga bowing her head before the God who had captured her heart, is immortalized in a miniature painting accompanying the Chronicle of Ioannis Skilitis, with the note,

 "The ruler of the Rus, a woman named Helga, who came to the Emperor Constantine and was baptized."

In this *Chronicle*, she is drawn in a special headdress "as a

newly-baptized Christian and honored deaconess of the Russian Church." Next to her was baptized a young woman named Malusha, who later became the mother of St. Vladimir. It should be noted Constantine VII was no fan of the Rus. It must have been difficult to induce him to become the godfather of Olga. The Russian Chronicles wax poetic about Olga's conversations with the Emperor, in which his counselors are amazed at her probing mind and spiritual maturity. In any case, she did manage to convince the proud Greeks that the Rus would be capable of taking on and absorbing the genius of Christian spirituality and culture. In this way, Olga was able to "conquer" Constantinople more completely than any of her military forefathers.

Constantine VII, a prolific writer, actually left an account of Olga's reception at court. He describes the majestic throne of the emperor with its mechanical singing bronze birds and roaring lions that accosted the incoming embassy of the Rus, which numbered 108 people. Then he wrote about the more intimate meetings in the chamber of the Empress, as well as the official feast in the hall of Justinian.

A DISAPPOINTING END

Diplomatically speaking, however, Olga's trip was not quite successful. She was unable to secure a dynastic marriage of Sviatoslav with one of Constantine's daughters. Nor was she able to get the Greeks to agree to an establishment of a Metropolitan's see in Kiev.

Her disappointments continued when she returned home. She tried to convince Sviatoslav to convert, but he was a confirmed pagan. He worshiped Perun, the Slavic counterpart to Thor, and refused to abandon his military faith. Their relationship began to cool after her conversion.

Unperturbed, Olga began a project of building churches in Rus. She founded the great Church of the Wisdom of God in

Kiev soon after her return from Constantinople. It was consecrated on May 11, 960. This day is still commemorated as a feast day of the Russian Church. The most important holy relic in the church was a cross she received at her baptism. On it was engraved the phrase:

> The land of Rus is renewed by the Holy Cross, accepted by Olga, the noble princess."

However, her Christian zeal angered some among the elites, who were still pagan. They looked with hope at Sviatoslav, who resented his mother's attempts to convert him. By this time, he was around twenty years old. His pagan entourage managed to remove Olga from any influence in the government of the Rus. Sviatoslav took all power to himself. He even killed some Christians and destroyed some of the churches Olga built.

It must have been difficult for Olga, who was so active and intelligent, to be relegated to the women's quarters. However, she was still respected. Whenever Sviatoslav went on a military campaigns (which he did often), she took over as regent. However, there was now no possibility of even considering a large-scale conversion to Christianity, which upset Olga greatly.

As she grew old and sickly, Olga, who had been baptized by one of the greatest dignitaries of the Christian church, was forced to keep a priest by her side in secret, lest she inspire a new wave of persecutions against Christians. She was buried in the Christian rite, having forbidden that any pagan feasts be performed in her honor.

She didn't manage to see it during her life, but her efforts were instrumental in her grandson's decision to unify the Rus under Christianity, a decision that did indeed lead to a flowering of a nation. Eventually, Rus took the reins of Christendom in the East from the Greeks. This "Third Rome" lasted until the twentieth century.

❧ 3 ❧

HOW ALEXANDER THE GREAT
BECAME POPULAR IN OLD
RUSSIA

I n keeping with the theme of history and myth being
intertwined in the early centuries of Russian history, there
was one surprising ruler that the Russians loved more than
all others. Not Oleg, not any half-legendary Viking ruler. No,
one of the most well-loved historical figures in Medieval Russia
was, of all people, Alexander the Great!

In the Middle Ages, a certain work called *Alexandria* was
widely popular. It was purported to be written by a certain
Callisthenes of Olynthus, a historian who accompanied
Alexander on his Asiatic expedition, and a nephew of Aristotle.
This "history" included many mythical events praising the greatness of the godlike Alexander. One episode in particular stuck in
early Russians' minds.

In a certain far Eastern country, Alexander saw two huge
birds. They awed him with their power and beauty. He
commanded that the birds be caught. He tied them to a basket,
sat in it, and began to fly up to heaven. In his hands, he held a
spear. On the end of the spear a piece of meat dangled, just out
of reach of the carnivorous birds. They kept trying to get at the
meat, and he kept on flying higher and higher. Alexander flew
upward for two days. Finally, on the third day, a bird of paradise

met him and spoke in a human voice: "You who yet know nothing earthly, how can you know the heavenly?"

Frightened by this encounter, Alexander hurried to fly back to earth.

This episode was so popular in Russia that it was etched on coins, used on princes' official seals, and was a popular decorative motif on jewelry. But the most striking example of its use is a carving on the Cathedral of St. Dmitry in Vladimir.

THE SYMBOLISM OF ASCENSION

What can explain this extraordinary popularity? It's hard to say. Perhaps the more important question is this: how did a pagan hero become so accepted by a Christian culture? He was so universally popular that a certain metropolitan of Kiev had the ascension of Alexander actually painted on his miter! The story did change a bit to better fit the Christian context. Instead of birds, the Russian version had gryphons. From ancient times, gryphons were symbolic creatures, guides of soul from this world into the next.

In Christian iconography, gryphons sometimes symbolized the two natures of Christ. They were visual representations of spiritual transformation, and they were also associated with the ascension of Christ. So their inclusion in this story makes Alexander's ascent a kind of "pagan prophecy" of Christ's ascension into heaven. Alexander was worthy to raise human nature to the divine, so he came back down and was humbled by the experience. It took the Incarnate God to take the fallen race of human beings and raise them up to the right hand of the Father in heaven.

THE IDEALIZED MONARCH

Others believe that the image of Alexander ascendant is an idealized image of the sacred nature of monarchy. It is true that in many societies, Alexander is prized as the ideal king, and many Russian princes honored and idolized him. Few know that even so venerable a person as St. Alexander Nevsky had planned to build a monastery in Pereslavl-Zalesskii dedicated to Alexander the Great, a pagan king!

It didn't end up happening, but Alexander's hold on the Russian imagination continued for centuries. This fact is beautifully reflected in the recent novel by Evgenii Vodolazkin, *Laurus*, where one of the main characters regularly quotes the *Alexandria* in almost the same hushed tones reserved for scripture.

❧ 4 ❧

HOW RUSSIA THREW OFF THE TATAR YOKE

It was late autumn, 1480 AD. Russian warriors, under the command of Grand Prince Ivan III, stood on the banks of the River Ugra. Shrouded in fog, freezing from the early winter cold, they waited. The other bank was teeming with the forces of their centuries-old enemies, the Tatars. Soon everyone would know that today was the end of three hundred years of humiliation. Today, Rus would throw off the Tatar yoke.

THE INSULT

The conflict between Grand Prince Ivan III of Moscow and Ahmad, Khan of the Great Horde, began with the usual problem— taxes. Apparently, Ivan III had had enough of paying tribute to the declining Khaganate. However, it's possible that the Khan did receive his tribute, but attacked Ivan III anyway, since the Grand Prince didn't bring the tribute in person, which would have been a terrible insult. However, it was also a political gamble. Technically, Ivan III had not yet received the grant of rule (*yarlyk*) that every Khan "gifted" to the Grand Prince of Moscow.

By not coming in person to the khan, Ivan III tacitly challenged the authority and power of the khan.

To add insult to injury, Ahmad sent an embassy to Moscow to insist on back payments of the previous princes' tributes. Again, Ivan III failed to show due deference to the representatives of the Khan. According to the "History of Kazan," he did more than that:

The Grand Prince was not afraid. He took the *basma* (a seal with the image of the Khan), spit on it, broke it, threw it on the ground, and stomped it with his feet."

(A recent Russian miniseries wasn't content with this level of drama, so the filmmakers have Ivan chopping off the Tatar ambassador's hand, which was highly unlikely.)

HESITATION

Although he challenged the khan, Ivan III refused to take decisive military action. History would validate his choice, but his contemporaries were less lenient. According to the Chronicles, Ivan III simply panicked. The people of Moscow took to the streets, loudly proclaiming that he was putting everyone in mortal danger through his indecision. Ivan III, fearing assassination, even left the city! His heir, Ivan the Younger, who was with the army, refused his father's repeated messages to leave the army and join him in hiding.

The situation was further complicated by the usual Russian problem. Ivan's brothers decided that it was time to challenge their brother's pretentions to power. It seemed that the internecine conflicts that had kept the Russians under the thumb of the Tatars for centuries would once again flare up, and at the most inappropriate time.

Finally, the Livonian Order picked this moment to attack Pskov with an army so powerful against the Russians, that no master of the order had ever gathered such an army, either before or after:

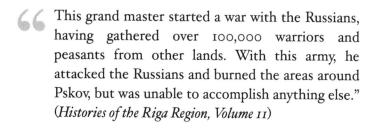

> This grand master started a war with the Russians, having gathered over 100,000 warriors and peasants from other lands. With this army, he attacked the Russians and burned the areas around Pskov, but was unable to accomplish anything else."
> (*Histories of the Riga Region, Volume 11*)

THE WAR BEGINS

Taking advantage of Moscow's tenuous position, Khan Ahmad scouted the right bank of the River Oka, and by autumn, he attacked with his main force:

> That year, the nefarious king Ahmad attacked Orthodox Christianity in Rus, attacked the holy churches and the Grand Prince, boasting that he would destroy all the holy churches and enslave all the Orthodox, even the Grand Prince, so that he would be no better off than the princes under Batu-Khan."

Finally overcoming his indecision, Ivan III gathered his forces and awaited news about the khan's movements in Kolomna, near Moscow. That same day, the Vladimir Icon of the Mother of God arrived to boost the morale of the warriors. This famous icon was believed to have saved Rus from total destruction at the hands of Tamerlane's army in 1395.

When Ivan III heard that the khan was planning to enter Russian lands by crossing the river Ugra, he sent part of his forces to hold the Tatars off until the main force of the Russians could arrive. Surprisingly, the khan didn't attack. Instead, he hoped to use a tactic that had worked before—to scare off the Russians merely by the size of his army.

THE STAND-OFF ON THE UGRA

On September 30, 1480, Ivan returned to Moscow for a final council with the Duma and the metropolitan of Moscow. He received a unanimous response:

 To stand firmly for Orthodox Christianity against the infidels."

That same day, his brothers came to him and declared that they would no longer stand against him. Ivan forgave them and commanded them to join the forces at the Ugra. Ivan himself entrenched in Kremenets nearby. The Russian line extended along the bank of the Ugra for 60 versts (almost forty miles!).

The first Tatar attempt to cross the Ugra occurred in early October, but they were quickly fought off. On October 8, the Khan himself tried to storm the Ugra, but Ivan the Younger's forces beat him back:

And the Tatars came and began to shoot at the Muscovites, but the Muscovites began to shoot back at them. They killed many with both arrows and cannons, and drove them back from the shores."

Over the next few days, the Tatars continued their attacks, but the Russian artillery barrages turned out to be too strong. Eventually, the Tatars retreated to the other shore, and the "Great Stand-off on the Ugra" began, with each side manning the opposite banks, waiting for an attack.

WHAT ABOUT THE POLISH KING?

The chief ally of Ahmad was the Grand Prince of Poland-Lithuania, Kasimir IV. Although at previous moments in history, and in future centuries, Polish rulers never passed up the opportunity to attack their Russian "brothers," Kasimir didn't come to the Ugra to help the Tatars.

Why not? Some historians believe that Kasimir had his own problems with the Tatars, and was fighting off the invasion of the Khan of Crimea. Others suggest that he was dealing with internal political problems. Furthermore, many Russians still living in Lithuania wanted to unite with the Grand Princedom of Muscovy. They may have influenced the king to avoid the conflict altogether.

In any case, Khan Ahmad waited for help from both Crimea and Poland, but all he got was the Russian winter.

Around October 20, Ivan III received a fiery letter from Vassian, archbishop of Rostov, who urged Ivan to emulate his brave ancestors:

> They not only protected the Russian lands from the infidels, but they even conquered other lands! Be brave and do not waver, my spiritual son, as a brave warrior of Christ. Follow the great words of our Lord in the Gospel. You are the good shepherd. The good shepherd gives his life for his sheep."

THE END OF THE CONFLICT

By the end of the month, Khan Ahmad had gathered all his forces, leaving no one to protect the Golden Horde, the headquarters of the Tatar power in Russia. Ivan III, surprised by this chance, gathered a small, elite force of warriors headed by Prince Vasilii the "Big-Nostriled." They slipped behind Tatar lines and harassed their holdings near the Horde.

Ivan himself was forced to change tactics. Stores were low, winter was coming fast. He concentrated his entire army at Borovsk, preparing for a decisive battle.

By that time, the khan heard about the elite Russian forces harassing the Horde. He sent some of his warriors back. By November 11, he made the final decision to abandon the field of battle and retreated completely.

To a contemporary eyewitness, it must have been a strange, even mystical scene. Two massive forces, primed for a battle the likes of which Rus hadn't seen in a hundred years. Suddenly, both retreat from the field of battle. The Russians ascribed this to the help of the Mother of God. Once again she had saved the Russian land from destruction. After that, the River Ugra began to be called "the girdle of the Mother of God."

Soon afterward, Ahmad was killed in an attack by a rival faction (probably with the secret support of Ivan III). This moment is generally considered the birth of the independent Russian-Muscovite state.

✻ 5 ✻

THE LAST PIRATES OF OLD RUS

I f you were to ask what people associated with Russia, you might get a host of answers. Nowadays, "hackers" would probably be on the top of the list. What people probably won't say is "pirates." But they'd be wrong . Most Russians themselves don't even know about Ushkuiniki. But they had a brief and exciting existence, the last shreds of a wild time before Russia was unified under a single city and ruler.

USHKUINIKI, THE LAST RUSSIAN PIRATES

Of all the cities of medieval Russia, Novgorod was one of the more volatile, not least because of its "semi-democratic" system of government. It's possible that the lack of a strong central authority caused the rise of an independent society of free pirates, called "Ushkuiniki." Their name (from the Russian "uzkii," thin) probably came from their boats. They were thin and very fast. Capable of seating around thirty raiders, they were light enough to make portage easy. The figurehead carved on the boats was often a polar bear.

Yes, if you guessed "are these Vikings?" you'd be partly right. They were the direct descendants of Vikings, both in terms of their ethnicity and their methods. The raiders worked in small, well-armed, and very well-trained military bands (*druzhyni*). Each had a single boat and would independently raid various cities, some at great distances from their "home base." Some went as far as the Arctic Sea and the borders of Mongol-controlled China.

Although there were Ushkuiniki all over the Russian north, they were especially prevalent around Novgorod (not least because of its importance as a trading post). Novgorod, unlike other cities, tolerated them for a time, even trying to channel the energy of the "young men," as they were jokingly called, to increase the influence of Novgorod over the other independent cities.

ORIGINS

Ushkuiniki may have begun raiding Bulgaria, Lithuania, and Scandinavia as early as the 11th century. They made their money primarily in the fur trade, the real money-maker of that time. They not only stole furs, but they controlled the riverways along the Kama and the Volga, raiding up and down along important trading posts. Some of them were strong enough to overcome entire cities, as we see from the overrunning of Koksharov in 1181.

They were thus important political players in the region as well. After all, the Russian fur trade extended as far as England through the Hanseatic League. Novgorod, seeking to control as much of the trade as possible, was more than willing to use the raiders to further its political goals, even if they never officially sanctioned them. It was a mutually beneficial "arrangement".

ARMS

Ushkuiniki were extremely well armed and provisioned. These professional warriors wore large-ring chain mail or scale mail that was very effective at warding off wide arrowheads. Each raider had his own sword and spear, and they used both longbows and crossbows effectively.

POLITICS

The Ushkuiniki were savvy political players as well. They often acted as mercenaries in the many internecine wars of the early Rus period. They were among the first to perceive how the Tatar power from the Golden Horde began to weaken, and they were very effective at determining the more politically and militarily strong party in any conflict, eagerly hiring themselves out to that party.

Here's an example. In 1360, they took a city in Bulgaria, and the annoyed Mongols asked the local Russian princes to take care of the raider problem. The princes managed to capture a few raiders in Kostroma and send them to the Golden Horde for execution. Kostroma lived to regret its involvement.

When Moscow and Tver were involved in their death struggle in the 14th century, Prokop, an Ushkuinik leader, was given carte blanch by the Moscow authorities, in return for his help in putting down Tver. Prokop began by avenging his fellow raider. He attacked Kostroma, destroying a 5,000-man army with only 1,000 strong. He took all the city's valuables and burned the city to the ground, taking the women and children and selling them into slavery.

Then Prokop's bands rampaged up and the down the Volga, going as far as Astrakhan, where they were only defeated by the favored "Eastern" method. That is, they were fed and given drink by "friends," then stabbed in their beds as they slept.

THE LAST RAID OF THE USHKUINIKI

The last raid of these Russian Vikings was a successful attack of 250 narrow boats on various Tatar strongholds along the Volga, led by a half-legendary warrior named Anfal Nikitin. He was a Novgorod nobleman who had become a vassal of Moscow and tried to take Novgorod for himself. He lost, and began to gather dispossessed raiders to himself, even establishing a city for them. We don't know what happened to Anfal, but he was probably killed by one of his own.

After his death, the Ushkuiniki began to fade, though they did take part as mercenaries in some famous battles. They continued to be a thorn in the side of the legitimate authorities until, in 1489, Ivan III permanently disbanded them. The remaining bands scattered, eventually falling into obscurity.

Interestingly, their leaders were called "Vatamans," which is a precursor to the Cossack leader's title of "Ataman," and may be etymologically related to the English "waterman."

❧ 6 ❧

THE CURSE OF THE MURDERED
PRINCE DMITRY OF UGLICH

I f Princess Olga's life reads like an adventure novel, then there are other episodes from Russian history that would fit well in a book of fairy tales. One of the more interesting of these is the so-called "curse of Prince Dmitry." Though Dmitry is a venerated as a saint in the Orthodox Church, from a historical point of view, his life reads more like a mystery than a life of a saint.

It began in October 1582, when Ivan the Terrible had a son named Dmitry, who had the unfortunate fate of being the last of the Riurikid dynasty (in the male line). According to the officially recognized history, he lived only eight years, but the curse of Prince Dmitry hung over Russia for over twenty-two years more.

ALARM BELLS IN UGLICH

Everything ended for the last son of Ivan the Terrible on May 25, 1591, in Uglich. Around midday, Prince Dmitry was playing a game of throwing knives with other children. In the official papers collected after his death, we read the following eye-witness account from one of the boys:

Prince Dmitry was playing at knives in the back courtyard, and suddenly he was struck with a fit, and he fell on his own knife."

This account was the only proof needed to officially announce the death an accident. However, no official word could possibly convince the residents of Uglich. Russians in the late Medieval era believed in signs and miracles much more eagerly than any logical conclusions of mere mortals. And there *was* a sign, and then some!

Immediately after Prince Dmitry's heart stopped beating, the great alarm bell of Uglich rang loudly. That in itself is nothing special, except local legend has it that the bell rang of its own accord. For several generations after this event, the people of Uglich continued to believe that this was an evil omen.

As soon as news spread of the prince's death, the locals rioted. They broke into the local offices of the Treasury and killed the clerk and his entire family. The powerful boyar Boris Godunov, who was the de facto ruler of Russia during the reign of the weak-willed Tsar Feodor Ioannovich, sent a detachment of riflemen to put down the riot.

It wasn't merely the locals who were punished for the riot. The alarm bell was as well. Its tongue was torn out, its "ear" was cut down, and it was publicly lashed twelve times in the city square. Then the humiliated bell was sent off with the rest of the rioters to Siberia. The local ruler of Tobolsk in Siberia ordered the bell to be locked up in a special cell, with a special sign over the door: "the inanimate first rioter from Uglich." (You can't make this stuff up!)

THE END OF THE RURIKID DYNASTY

As soon as news of Prince Dmitry's death spread to the rest of Russia, the rumors started. Immediately, people suspected Boris Godunov's hand in the "accidental death." However, there were others who suspected Tsar Feodor himself in the murder. And there were reasons to think so.

Forty days after Ivan IV's death, Feodor, his heir, began to actively plan his coronation. One week before his coronation, he ordered that Prince Dmitry and his mother (Ivan's sixth wife) be effectively banished to Uglich. This was obviously a terrible insult to the dead tsar's family. However, Feodor did not stop there.

For example, only a few months after he began ruling, he officially ordered the clergy to remove Dmitry's name from the list of liturgical commemorations. The ostensible reason was that Prince Dmitry was the product of a sixth (and ecclesiastically unrecognized) marriage. But some saw this as nothing more than an excuse. There were more than a few who assumed this cessation of commemoration to be essentially a death wish.

A British traveler named Fletcher reported during his travels of 1588-1589 that Dmitry's wet-nurse died of poisoning. Many whispered that the poison had been intended for the prince instead.

THE CURSE BEGINS

Six months after Prince Dmitry died, Feodor's wife, Irina Godunova, conceived. Everyone eagerly awaited an heir, and various legends tell that every possible wizard and soothsayer in the court promised a son. Instead, a daughter was born, named Feodosia. As soon as she was born, the rumors began. The people whispered that she was born exactly one year after the death of Dmitry, and the official announcement of her birth was delayed a month for that reason.

But this wasn't the worst omen. The girl only lived for a few months before she died. And here, for the first time, we begin to hear of the curse of Prince Dmitry. Tsar Feodor changed after the death of his daughter. He lost all interest in the ruling of his country and began to spend months on end in monasteries. Some people said that he was trying to atone for his guilt in killing the innocent Prince Dmitry. Tsar Feodor Ioannovich died in 1598, leaving no heir.

THE GREAT FAMINE

The death of the last Riurikid opened the door to the rule of Tsar Boris Godunov. By this time, the common people attached the epithet of "prince-killer" to Godunov's name. This, however, didn't bother him too much. Through a series of shrewd political moves, he assumed the throne and immediately began reforming the government. In two years, he enacted more changes than all the tsars of the 16th century.

Just as it seemed that he had gained the love of the people, a catastrophe struck Russia. A series of natural disasters led to a horrifying famine that lasted three years. The historian Karamzin wrote:

 People ate grass like cattle; people found hay in the mouths of the dead. Horseflesh was considered a delicacy. People ate dogs, cats, carcasses, all sort of filth. People became worse than animals. They left their wives and families just to avoid sharing the last bit of food. People did not only rob each other, or kill for a bit of bread, but people cannibalized each other. Human meat was sold in markets inside pies!"

In Moscow alone, 120,000 people died. Bands of outlaws ravaged the countryside. Whatever love had appeared for the new tsar died with the famine. Once again, people remembered the curse of Prince Dmitry and called Boris "the accursed one."

THE END OF THE SHORT-LIVED GODUNOV DYNASTY

The year 1604 finally had a good harvest. It seemed that things might go back to normal. But it was only the calm before the storm. In late 1604, Godunov found out that an army was gathering in Poland, led by a man who called himself Prince Dmitry, as though the prince had miraculously avoided his killers in Uglich back in 1591. Now, Godunov was called "the slave tsar," and everyone awaited the return of the beloved prince.

Godunov never met False Dmitry. He died in 1605, a few months before the fake prince's triumphal "return". The curse of Dmitry did not end for the Godunov family with Boris's death. His son Feodor and his wife were smothered to death shortly before the false Dmitry's arrival in Moscow.

THE END OF THE PEOPLE'S TRUST

The false Dmitry never managed to "restore" the Riurikid dynasty. A group of boyars, led by Vasili Shuiskii, organized a coup and killed the false Dmitry. They officially announced to the people that the returned hero prince was actually an imposter, and his dead body was publicly humiliated for good measure.

This absurd display completely ended the people's trust in the government. The commoners refused to believed that the prince was an imposter, and they lamented his death bitterly. And nature seemed to concur. That summer, an unusual freeze hit Moscow, and it destroyed that year's harvest completely. The curse of Prince Dmitry took on new life. People began to tell of various miraculous appearances of the martyred prince.

Afraid of the rise of a cult around the murdered false prince, Shuiskii had his body disinterred, burned, and fired out of a cannon in the direction of Poland.

THE END OF VASILI SHUISKII

Vasili Shuiskii had been the boyar in charge of the official investigation into the young Prince Dmitry's death in Uglich in 1591. He was the one who officially announced that the boy's death was an accident. But as soon as he took over and became Tsar himself, he changed his mind and declared that, actually, Boris Godunov had murdered the young prince. By doing this, Shuiskii killed two birds with one stone. He discredited his dead predecessor and showed that the "new Dmitry" was, in fact, an impostor.

He decided to finalize the latter truth by arranging a committee to investigate the possibility of glorifying the killed prince as a saint. Metropolitan Philaret (Romanov) of Rostov headed a group of investigators who traveled to Uglich. They disinterred the body and were shocked to find an incorrupt child's body that began to smell sweetly as soon as they uncovered it. Not only that, but in those fifteen years, his clothing, a handkerchief in his left hand, and even a few nuts that the boy still clutched in his right hand were all untouched by rot.

Most telling of all was the fact that his neck had clearly been slashed open.

The relics were triumphantly brought to the Kremlin, and the crowds gathered to venerate the child-saint. Eyewitness accounts of miracles began to be recorded almost immediately, especially healing from blindness. (Interestingly, a famous painting by Nesterov depicts the prince with his eyes closed, as though he didn't need his eyes any more.)

The after-effects, so to speak, of the curse of Prince Dmitry continued for years. Various other impostors pretending to be Dmitry appeared on the scene, and the Time of Troubles left Russia at the mercy of Catholic Poland. However, Metropolitan Philaret's role in Dmitry's canonization and the development of his veneration effectively sealed the future fate of a successfully restored Russian monarchy. His son Michael became the first Romanov tsar. It's almost as though Prince Dmitry, finally at rest, blessed the rise of the new dynasty that would see Russia become a major political and cultural player in the world.

A HERO FOR ANY TIME

Heroism. Heroes. We want to believe in them. But too often, both in history and current events, it seems the heroes have headed for the hills, leaving the halls of power to the cunning and the unscrupulous. And so we indulge in escapist fantasies about superheroes that might save us from ourselves, if they can get their own lives in order first, that is.

In my writer's manifesto, I describe what I see as a necessary "story hero" for our time. He is not a hulking warrior who puts down hundreds of enemies with his sword. He is not a cunning politician who outwits his corrupt fellows to help further yet another social program. No Conan, no Odysseus. Instead, he is a man of humility, yet a man of strength. (I should say that whatever I say of heroes is true of heroines as well).

As difficult as it is to find such heroes in fiction, it's even more difficult to find them in history, especially during the tumultuous time when Prince Dmitry was murdered. But it seems that the best heroes are made in the crucible of dark times. Interestingly enough, one such hero, a true hero for any time, was also a Prince Dmitry. But his last name was Pozharky.

A MILITARY FAMILY

The Pozharsky family was descended from Riurik, the half-legendary first ruler of the Rus. In the 16th century, the family fell into decline and lost its ancestral holdings. In those days, there were several ways for a noble family to gain status:

- Appointment to a military command
- Assignment as a city governor
- Presence at court
- Ideally, a seat in the Boyar Duma, the circle of advisors to the Tsar.

To get into the Duma, however, you had to receive a special rank from the Grand Prince of Moscow himself.

In the 16th century, scores of aristocratic families campaigned to achieve "Duma" status. Hundreds more vied for military commander postings. The Pozharsky family showed no such ambitions, content to merely be useful. They received low-level assignments in the army.

Many of them lost their lives in various battles. They never achieved Boyar or Duma status, despite their noble birth. And when one of them rose to a slightly higher social position, that Pozharsky was always happy to serve, even if that service took him somewhere to the remotest outskirts of the country.

It's interesting to me that a man who would become the savior of Russia came from relatively humble, if hardworking, stock.

INTO THE FIRE OF THE TIMES OF TROUBLE

Prince Dmitry entered the so-called Time of Troubles (1598-1613) as a middle-rank officer, something between colonel and major general in our terms. This was considered a decent career for those times, better than most of Dmitry's ancestors. Still, it was nothing spectacular. In spite of this, he became one of the most remarkable figures of the short, but bloody, Time of Troubles.

During the reign of Tsar Vasily Shuisky (1606 – 1610), Pozharsky finally became a first-rank military commander (voyevoda). He was an effective commander, defending the capital from Polish-Lithuanian gangs and Russian rioters alike. Shuisky, one of the least popular Tsars in Russian history, failed to control a rising tide of ill feeling against him. It didn't help that a man pretending to be a murdered heir of the Riurikid line, the first so-called False Dmitry, was gaining support among all levels of society as he marched on Moscow with a Polish army.

In 1610, Pozharsky was serving as voyevoda of Zaraisk, a town near Moscow. It was besieged by an army of Russians who believed in the right of False Dimitri to the throne of Moscow. In this frightening atmosphere of treachery, when one couldn't tell friend from foe, Pozharsky managed to keep his own army loyal to the Tsar, remaining steadfast inside the kremlin of Zaraisk. Eventually, though he was besieged, he managed to put the rebellion down.

However, in that same year, the Russian aristocracy, having decided that it preferred to rule the country on their own, betrayed Tsar Vasily Shuisky. Lulled into false security by spurious promises of the Polish government, they invited an army of Polish invaders into Moscow. They believed they could take control of the political turmoil and get rid of autocracy in favor of an oligarchy. Instead, they betrayed their country and made it a vassal state of Poland. It was a moment of terrible, unbearable humiliation for Russia.

Despite False Dmitry's temporary success in taking Moscow, he still needed to secure his military position. He invited Ukrainian Cossacks to Moscow to support his own Polish troops. Before they could reach Moscow, Pozharsky's army and a guerilla force led by Prokopii Liapunov managed to clear them out of the areas near Ryazan. Then, both of the victorious Russian armies moved toward Moscow. Pozharsky got there first.

THE FIGHT FOR MOSCOW

It didn't take long for a rebellion to break out inside Moscow itself. The Muscovites could no longer bear the oppression, thievery, and humiliation at the hands of the Polish garrison. The fight for the city was merciless and violent. The Poles stormed Russian barricades, while the barricade defenders shot at Poles from guns and cannons.

The last stronghold of Russian resistance was a simple wooden fortification built on the orders of Pozharsky near the Church of the Meeting of the Lord on Sretenka. The Poles couldn't take his position. Instead of losing Moscow, they preferred to burn it down. A horrible fire consumed the greater part of the capital. Pozharsky himself was heavily wounded, and his rebellion stagnated.

However, an army, gathered from various cities near Moscow, arrived to help the rebels. For more than a year, they remained near the ruins of the capital, intermittently fighting the invaders to a stalemate. Dmitry Pozharsky was evacuated from the city.

THE LIBERATOR

The autumn of 1611 was possibly the worst year in Russian history. There was no government to speak of. The ostensible rulers of Russia were a gang of traitors who occupied the Kremlin and tried to rule the country with foreign soldiers. Ravaging Cossacks burned down cities and villages all over the countryside, robbing and killing as they went. The Swedish army captured the entire Russian North, even going so far as Novgorod.

The Polish king crossed the border and his troops camped near Smolensk. He sent reinforcements to the Polish garrison in Moscow.

At such a moment, the entire history of Russia teetered on the edge of a knife. It would have been very easy to give up, to capitulate, to abandon Russia's future for temporary gain. But mustering all that remained of its strength, Pozharsky's small resistance army remained standing on the ashes of the capital. However, without him there, the commanders couldn't stop quarreling among themselves.

Russia was on the verge of a permanent collapse, never to revive. But then, something changed.

A few wealthy cities remained unoccupied by Polish invaders. Among these, Kazan and Nizhny Novgorod were an epicenter for the liberation movement. A new army began to rally at Nizhny Novgorod, then gathered troops and supplies throughout the region until it reached Yaroslavl.

In Yaroslavl, a "provisional government" was organized, which included a Council of the Land with government offices and even its own mint. Yaroslavl essentially became the Russian capital for a time.

The Charter of the Council of the Lands began with the words: "By the order of the Moscow State, the boyars and the governors, and the steward and voevoda Prince Dmitry Mikhailovich Pozharsky."

To be thus singled out among all other noblemen was a great honor, but Pozharsky was not a seeker for power. He was a skilled military commander, but so were many others. What set him apart was his reputation for honesty and integrity, as well as incredible courage. He had never grabbed money for himself. He had never taken advantage of the confused political situation to advance his own family's humble prospects.

And the commoners were ready to follow him, despite his noble standing. There was almost no one else to trust, except for the humble, yet adamantine war leader.

Russia did not have a Tsar, but Prince Pozharsky assumed many of his functions. The persistent Nizhny Novgorod citizens and Smolensk noblemen, who were the nucleus of the new army, insisted that he needed to lead them. Pozharsky had not yet recovered from his wounds and was leery of betrayal.

However, he agreed to take command of the army after long negotiations.

In July 1612, the vanguard of this new liberation army arrived in Moscow. By August 20, the main force had also arrived. From the west, the traitor Cossack Hetman Khodkevich's powerful armies swooped swiftly towards the city. The collision with him would decide the fate of the Russian capital.

What view met Prince Pozharsky's eyes when he returned to Moscow? Black fires, smoking churches, burnt-out hulks of buildings here and there, stained with ashes. However, some business-minded Muscovites had managed to build themselves new "mansions" among the rubble.

The soldiers of Pozharsky's first rebel army, which he was forced to abandon when wounded, had made themselves dugouts, occupying the surviving houses. They lived in persistent hunger. Only the walls of the ancient Kremlin, crippled by artillery fire, towered over the ruins ...

Pozharsky had a very small number of well-armed, truly battle-worthy cavalry from the nobility as well as a small section of Tatar cavalry at his disposal. The bulk of the troops were foot soldiers. As an experienced leader, the prince knew that the Russian infantry of that time rarely showed steadfastness at the time of battle. But on the defensive, it was almost unbreakable.

Give a dozen Russian sharpshooters not just a stone wall, but even a few overturned wagons, and they would keep off hundreds of enemies. So, Pozharsky decided to build wooden fortifications inside the city as strong points, and then to dig trenches. He planned to combine the defensive tactics of the infantry with cavalry offensives.

This tactic brought him success in a persistent three-day battle.

On August 22, Pozharsky's cavalry attacked the Poles and Cossacks around the Novodevichy Convent. The Poles threw in massive forces into the battle, and the Russian cavalry retreated, but was able to regain its bearings at a small wooden fortification near the Arbat Gate. Here, Khodkevich threw his reserves into the fray. Nevertheless, the Cossacks could not shake the Russian soldiers from the position they had occupied.

The persistent confrontation with the hardened soldiers of Khodkevich made the outcome of the battle more and more ambiguous. But a sudden strike from the detachments of the first rebel militia, who finally came to aid their comrades in their hour of need, decided the matter: the Poles and Cossacks retreated.

However, on the night of August 22-23, aided by a Russian traitor, the Poles captured the small wooden fortification of the first rebel army. For no apparent good reason, Hetman Khodkevich took the entire next day to prepare for a decisive blow, giving the Russian liberation army a much-needed rest.

On August 24, the Poles pushed back the Russians, but they failed to break through the defense of the main forces. However, one of the militia regiments failed to hold a key fortification, and they allowed Khodkevich to break through into the center of Pozharky's lines. It looked again like Pozharsky would lose. But his forces suddenly counterattacked and drove the Poles back.

The fighting paused. The troops of both sides had suffered horrendous losses and were exhausted. Pozharsky realized that this moment was ideal for taking the initiative. He sent a detachment of several hundred fighters, led by the merchant Kusma Minin, to the Moscow River. The unexpected attack of the Russian forces, who the day before barely held their positions and seemed on the edge of collapse, took the Poles by surprise. Soon, their fighting spirit was broken, and the battle for Moscow turned.

It was the decisive last step that broke the invaders' backs. The next day, the enemy forces began to withdraw from Moscow.

The invaders still held the center of the city for a few more months. In November, the Russian militia stormed China-city. The Polish garrison surrendered soon afterward.

The peak of the Great Trouble had passed.

After the liberation of Moscow and the beginning of the reign of Tsar Mikhail Fedorovich (who ruled from 1613 to 1645), the first of the Romanov dynasty, Pozharsky was awarded the highest rank of boyar (1613), admitted to the Duma, and was given large estates. For him, a man seemingly inconspicuous in the ranks of the brilliant Moscow aristocracy, the boyar rank had been an unattainable dream.

SERVANT TO THE TSAR

Dmitri Mikhailovich was honored as a "great bogatyr", a military leader "skillful in war". He continued to take part in military operations. In 1615, Pozharsky defeated the soldiers of the famous Polish vagabond Lisovsky next to the city of Orlov. Leading 600 people against 2000, Pozharsky repelled the enemy, taking 30 captives, the enemy banners and drums. In autumn 1618, Pozharsky, a sick man barely alive from old wounds, served as the siege voevoda in Kaluga, harassing the Poles with constant attacks and eventually forcing the enemy to retreat from the city.

Even during the Smolensk War of 1632-1634, Pozharsky, exhausted by the "black ailment" (a serious illness), aged over 60, still led his soldiers tirelessly.

He funded the construction of the Kazan Cathedral on Red Square, which was destroyed in the Soviet era and rebuilt in the 1990's. Pozharsky donated generously to churches. He especially liked to buy expensive liturgical books for priests.

He died from complications from his wounds in 1642. Here is how historian Ivan Zabelin describes this hero for our time:

> You do not need particularly keen eyes to see Pozharsky's motives. He did not stand for personal goals and he did not serve any party. He served his people and his land, and he served them purely,

straightforwardly, and honestly. It was his ordinary deeds and actions that gave such a quotidian man a significance unusual for that time. It was this significance that the people in Nizhny Novgorod understood so well, when they wished to find a leader for the liberation movement who would not betray them all, who would not switch sides, searching for advantages for his own honor or for self-interest, as did the vast majority of the princes, boyars, and governors of the time."

How wonderful such an assessment sounds, and how necessary for our days! What's so amazing about his story is that he was only a single man, and not a very powerful one at that. And yet, his single-minded virtue and integrity moved mountains and changed the tide of a war no one thought he could win. That's a lesson any person can learn, especially when it seems that we can do nothing to shift the tide of injustice, corruption, and degradation in our own culture and political system.

⚜ 8 ⚜

A RUSSIAN CINDERELLA STORY

Sometimes, truth really is stranger than fiction. Take the story of Cinderella, the quintessential rags to riches story, the golden standard of the "fairy tale ending." Well, believe it or not, Russia had a historical Cinderella story, and at the highest levels of government. The setting, the characters, and the ending are almost too perfectly plotted to be historical.

THE SETTING

Russia, wounded and barely alive, had just emerged out of the most difficult period of its history. This "Time of Troubles" saw not one, but two tsars with dubious names of "False Dimitri." Rus's ancestral enemy, Poland, occupied the throne of Moscow. The capital city itself burned almost to the ground. Only by the slimmest of margins did a liberation army, under the command of a brilliant, self-effacing leader, manage to drive away the invader.

After the entire country unified to choose a new Tsar, Michael, the son of the Patriarch of Moscow Philaret, it seemed things might finally be on the mend for the beleaguered country.

But the specter of internecine war seemed to loom again when Tsar Michael was still unmarried at the ripe old age of thirty.

His father, Patriarch Philaret, couldn't arrange a wedding for his son, since he was languishing in a prison in Poland. So the job fell to the Patriarch's former wife, the nun Martha. (Why were the Tsar's parents both monastics? That's a story for a different day. But yes, unfortunately it had to do with political intrigue).

THE BEAUTY PAGEANT

In 1626, under the direction of Nun Martha, official decrees were sent to all Russian cities about the Tsar's need for a bride. She needed to be of a noble family, beautiful, and intelligent. Also considered necessary were tall height and good health (both apparently indicative of the ability to bear strong male heirs). Any and all who fit the bill were to report to the capital posthaste.

It wasn't easy for prospective brides to get into the exclusive "viewing of the bride". After undergoing what was effectively an old-time beauty pageant, only sixty young ladies were deemed worthy of the private viewing with the Tsar himself.

However, Tsar Michael, who was no slouch, did not find any of the sixty to be quite right. Half-legendary history tells that the Tsar couldn't see any natural beauty among them, since all of them were so carefully made up and dressed to the nines.

It is probable that a young man raised by a nun, with a bishop for a father, was well read in the classics of spiritual literature. It was almost as if he had St. John Chrysostom's stark words in his mind when he considered his future bride:

 Do you wish to adorn your face? Do not do so with gems but with piety and modesty; thus adorned, a man will find your appearance more pleasing to behold. For that other kind of adornment gives rise to suspicions which give rise to jealousy, enmity, strife, and quarrels."

So his mother offered to set up a secret contest to find the true beauty among them.

THE NIGHT INSPECTION

In the middle of the night, after everyone had fallen asleep, the mother and son walked with a candle through all the rooms of the sleeping brides. No makeup, no fancy hairdos, no hiding behind layers and layers of bejeweled clothing. And the Tsar made his choice.

His choice surprised everyone. She was not one of the sixty chosen candidates. Nor was she noble born. She had come to the Tsar's palace as a servant to one of the sixty! The court was shocked by the news that the Tsar had chosen a servant girl to be the Tsaritsa of Russia.

But it was just like a fairy tale. Her simple beauty, intelligence, and gentle bearing won the Tsar over. In spite of all the protests and the complaints of the boyars and even Nun Martha, Michael Romanov insisted. Now came the difficult part. The boyars, though they had just been punished severed for it by the Time of Troubles, couldn't quite part with their instinct to intrigue.

The young lady, Evdokia Streshneva, had to be guarded night and day. After all, it wasn't unheard-of for brides, in the weeks before their weddings, to develop strange maladies that proved them "unfit to bear children." Sometimes it was a bribed doctor, sometimes a cook who slipped something nasty into the young lady's food.

So Tsar Michael decided to dispense with formality completely. He married her three days after their announced betrothal. And it was this young lady, so removed from the nastiness of courtly intrigue, who gave birth to Tsar Alexei Mikhailovich, one of the most brilliant rulers Russia would ever have.

❧ 9 ❧

THE RUSSIAN DA VINCI

As we leave the medieval period, the boundary between legend and fact becomes much more defined. We've entered the period of the so-called enlightenment, when enchantment of all kind simply disappears (it was stamped out vehemently). I find this to be a sad development.

But there are still surprising moments and people that shine like fireflies in an otherwise brutal and disturbing time period (you know, Peter the Not-so-good, Catherine the Horrifying). One of these was a simple man who was more at home in a workshop than in the usual places where history is made.

When you think about the great inventors of history, a few names come up: Archimedes, Leonardo da Vinci, Galileo, Thomas Edison. Few of the "best of" lists include one of the greatest, however. His name was Ivan Kulibin, and he may have been the first inventor of the elevator.

Though not very well known (even among Russians), Ivan Kulibin was a true Renaissance man. Like da Vinci, some of his ideas have been developed into modern analogues in machine-building, medicine, and architecture.

Here are seven of the most surprising inventions of this Russian da Vinci.

THE "WATER-WALKER"

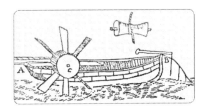

In 1804, Kulibin built a "water-walker," a motorized boat that could travel up the current. He first had his idea in childhood— as a child, he was moved by the heaviness of the labor of the Volga barge-men. From that moment in childhood, he dreamed of creating something that would make their life easier.

THE ARCHED BRIDGE

Kulibin designed a wooden one-arch bridge to cross the Neva river, spanning 298 meter (instead of the usual 50-60 meter spans), using a girder with a cross grate that he invented himself. A 1/10th size model was successfully tested in the Tavrichesky Garden in Petersburg. He even drew up designs for some of the earliest metal arched bridges in existence. Unfortunately, these projects were ultimately not financed by the government.

A SELF-DRIVING CARRIAGE

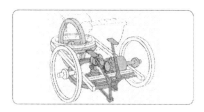

In 1791, Kulibin designed and built a carriage that was powered by a person pushing on pedals. More than that, he even designed it a gearbox, breaks, and a flywheel. The design for Kilibin's three-wheel self-driving carriage was used by Karl Benz when designing the first automobile.

THE FIRST ELEVATOR

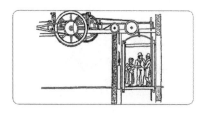

This elevator was invented for Catherine II personally. It was a small chair that rose up and down on winches and was used both as a source of the court's entertainment as well as the empress's personal comfort.

PROSTHETICS

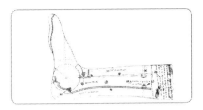

Kulibin perfected the system of prosthesis making. He created a "mechanical leg" for Lieutenant Sergei Nepeitsyn, who had lost his leg at war. From that point, Nepeitsyn was nick-named "metal leg," while Kulibin's design found wide distribution later in France when an entrepreneur found and developed Kulibin's design.

A CLOCK INSIDE AN EASTER EGG

In 1764-1767, Kulibin created a unique clock that he believed worthy of the attention of the empress herself. The clock's case was a golden Easter egg. The master clockmaker built into it a watch mechanism and a chiming mechanism, as well as an automated theatrical scene on a minuscule scale. Every hour, tiny figurines of the Myrrh-bearing Women and an angel played out the scene at the Tomb of Christ, to the chiming of "Christ is Risen." To put it together, Kulibin needed 427 details and five years of work. This clock can still be seen in the Hermitage Museum in St. Petersburg.

❧ 10 ❧

HOW NAPOLEON'S SOLDIERS
BECAME COSSACKS

One of the more interesting scenes in *Godfather II* is where young Vito is given the last name "Corleone" by the American border guard, only because he's from Corleone. It turns out that my own last name may have a similar kind of history (or legend). The story (fiction or history, who knows?) is that our Kotar ancestor was not really a Kotar at all, but he was from Kotor (Montenegro). In the early 19th century, he had the unfortunate fate of being in the path of Napoleon's armies.

Luckily, my Kotar ancestor was a doctor. Napoleon was no fool. He needed plenty of doctors, carpenters, metal-workers, and other professionals in his army. And he was not averse to "impressing" people into his army. So Dr. Kotar accompanied Napoleon on his fateful invasion of Russia.

We all know how that ended...

Well, Dr. Kotar wasn't the only one who ended up staying in Russian lands after Napoleon's failure. Some of Napoleon's soldiers did the unthinkable. They became Cossacks!

WHAT HAPPENED TO NAPOLEON'S ARMY AFTER DEFEAT?

In 1869, a French engineer named Charles-Joseph Minard decided to begin a unique project. He created a diagram in which he plotted the losses of Napoleon's armies during the Russian campaign. According to his research, 422,000 soldiers entered Russia with Napoleon. Only 10,000 returned to France.

Later research would show that Menard didn't include the over 200,000 (one of whom was Dr. Kotar) who were impressed into the army during the campaign. The newest research, however, is no less impressive. Of the over 600,000 person army that entered Russia, no more than 50,000 returned. At the same time, casualty reports account for no more than 150,000 deaths. What happened to the other 400,000?

The summer of 1812 was unseasonably hot. A significant amount of soldiers died from heatstroke and heart attacks related to the heat. The situation was not helped by the usual infections that plague any large army during the march. But the heat was quickly replaced by sudden cold and extreme rains that soon turned to snow.

Historian Vladlen Sirotkin believed that 200,000 of the French army were taken as prisoners of war. Many of them did not survive. All the same, almost 100,000 of them still remained in Russia two years after the end of the war, and of them, 60,000 became Russian citizens. After the end of the war, the restored Louis XVIII asked Alexander I to repatriate the French who remained in Russia, but Alexander I did nothing.

"FRENCH LEFTOVERS"

The proof of French habitation in Russia is seen all over the country. In Moscow, to this day, there are about twenty families who are descended from French soldiers. Oddly enough, the city with the largest population of these "French leftovers" is

Chelyabinsk in the Urals (literally the middle of nowhere). But more on that later.

Samara had a place called "The French Mill," presumably because French prisoners of war worked there. And near the city of Syktyvkar (Vologda region) stands a village called Paris. The legend goes that it was founded by French prisoners of war.

The Russian language also has plenty of "French leftovers." Hungry and cold French soldiers would sometimes ask Russian peasants for bread, addressing them as "chers amis" (dear friends). Whenever they asked for a horse, they used the French "cheval," naturally. Strangely enough, in Russian slang, "sharomizhnik" and "shval'" are words that mean "hobo" or "wandering bum."

NAPOLEONIC COSSACKS

Napoleon is said to have had a high opinion of Cossacks: "Give me the Cossacks alone, and I will take over Europe with them." Oddly enough, some of his own soldiers would end up joining that famed army. But the adaptation didn't happen overnight. Historians are still assembling much of this information.

For example, Professor Sirotkin found a small community of Napoleon's soldiers in the Altai (far Siberia). The documents show that three French soldiers—Vensan, Cambré, and Louis—willingly departed to the taiga, where they were given land and the designation of "local peasants."

Some officers were taken in by noble families of Russia. A certain under-lieutenant named Ruppel wrote a memoir of how he lived in the family of a nobleman of Orenburg named Plemiannikov. As for the nobles of Ufa, they became famous for their unceasing parties, dances, and hunts in honor of their French guests. They even fought each other for the privilege of inviting the invaders over for dinner!

In all of Orenburg, around 40 of these French officers ended up staying, and twelve of them showed an interest in entering the Cossack army. By the beginning of the 20th century, there were over 200 Cossacks with French roots in the Orenburg Cossack Division. As for the famed Don Cossack army, local historians found that at least 49 descendants of French soldiers had joined the army by the end of the 19th century. They weren't that easy to find, as it turned out. For example, "Jandre" changed his name to "Zhandrov", while "Billenon" became "Belov."

THE FRENCH "NEW FRONT"

In the beginning of the 19th century, the town of Verhneural'sk (in the Chelyabinsk region) was a small fort that defended the Southeastern borders of Russia against Kazakh incursions. In 1836, that area needed to be propped up, and so a new front of forts and military towns was built all along that border. From Omsk to Berezovk a chain of Cossack village-forts was built. Four of them had French names: Champenuaz, Arsi, Paris, and Brienne. All the "French Cossacks" in the area were relocated to these forts, together with their families.

The local Kazakh sultan, spooked by the move, decided to try to invade. And so Napoleon's old soldiers had to return to war, but for the army that used to be their enemy.

As for Dr. Kotar, he didn't join the Cossacks. He settled in Western Belarus (near Brest), where nearly all of his progeny became priests. There are still Kotars living in Brest to this day.

AS SURPRISING AS it might be to consider that Napoleon's famed soldiers might become Cossacks, the reality is that the Cossacks were a fascinating and attractive people. And as warlike as they were, their core value was the family unit.

The Cossacks considered it dishonorable to have uneducated sons, and they dreamed for happiness for their daughters. If a

Cossack were fated to go to his death in battle, the village would not leave his family to fend for themselves.

In the 17th century, the Don Cossacks were constantly at war. All questions were resolved by the village at large. Women were not involved in the running of the village, and initially they occupied a subordinate role. At that time, it was normal to marry Turkish, Persian, and Circassians girls taken as spoils of war. Historical records witness that in winter of 1635, the Cossacks brought back 1,735 captive women from their campaigns.

It happened also that Cossack women would be taken into slavery by the Crimean Tatars or Turks, but the Cossacks expended all possible energy and resources to free their women from the "busurmane" (heathen). Sometimes these rescues took years. As a rule, when these women were rescued, they already had Tatar children. It was traditional not to leave these former captives alone. The Cossacks married them and the half-Tatar children were accepted as their own.

In the 16th and 17th centuries, the public assemblies in each village had absolute power. This is why fathers who wanted worthy men as sons-in-law required the entire village to provide surety for their daughters' potential husband. A Cossack who gave his word at one of these assemblies always kept his word.

"Be my wife," said a young man to his desired bride.

"Be my husband," she answered him.

This proposal was done in public, at one of the aforementioned assemblies. If the Cossacks all decided that this was a good match, a new family was born. Divorce happened in the same way, and the husband always had to explain his reasoning and convince the entire village. Usually, another Cossack would then cover the divorced woman with the hem of his kaftan, as if to shield her from dishonor. In such cases, the woman would become his wife. But women could initiate divorce as well. If a woman's husband turned out to be a rake, the assembly would invariably choose in the woman's favor.

The Don Cossacks had a unique system of social self-organization. If a Cossack went to war, he could be sure that his children would lack for nothing if he died. However, this was true only of the families whose unions were ratified by the public assembly.

For example, let's say a rider comes to the village with bad news that an enemy had attacked the southern border of Russia, and it must be held at all cost until the full Don Cossack army can be mobilized. In such cases, the public assembly would gather. The ataman (military leader) would first take off his hat, then throw off his kaftan. This meant that the danger was extreme.

"Who wants to be hanged, impaled on a spike, or boiled in tar?" The ataman would ask. In answer, volunteers would come forward, knowing that they go to a sure death. Surrounded by total silence, they would ask the rest of the Cossacks:

"Who will take my orphans and my widow as his own?"

And there was always a Cossack who would swear a public oath: "I will take them as my own!"

In the eighteenth century, the role of women in Cossack villages grew more important. The historian V. D. Suhorukov believes this occurred as a result of the unusual beauty of Cossack women. The thing is, after centuries of marrying the women brought back as spoils of war, Cossacks were a mix of the most diverse ethnic groups, making the women especially beautiful. "Fiery black eyes, cheeks full of fresh life, perfect cleanliness and diligence in dress. They all loved to dress up and even applied rouge," wrote Suhorukov.

At the same time, the Cossack women were well known for their strong characters. The ethnographer G. B. Gubarev characterized them thus:

 Centuries of constant troubles formed in Cossack women a fearless determination. She was a good boatman, rode a horse with great skill, was greatly

adept with lassos and weapons. She was perfectly
capable of defending her children and her home."

Eventually the old saying "Hold both your horse and your
women by the reins" came to lose its original meaning in
Cossack society. Seeing such a decisive and capable beauty
before his eyes, the Cossack, whether he wished to or not, could
only have the greatest respect for her.

The Orthodox feast day of the Entry of the Mother of God
into the Temple on November 21 became for the Cossacks a
traditional celebration of the mother-Cossack. In essence, this
was the first "mother's day" in Russia. Not merely mothers, but
all Cossack women were celebrated.

Compared to Russian peasant families, Cossacks had few
children, and so every one of them was greatly loved. Since
Cossack life was fraught with dangers, parents were careful to
follow all the old traditions. For example, when the first tooth
began to cut through the gum, the parents ordered a service of
supplication to St. John the Warrior.

According to another tradition, a boy's first haircut was on
his first birthday, but his second was on his seventh birthday,
which indicated the end of childhood. From this age, he learned
to shoot, and from age ten he learned how to use a saber. From
age three, he learned how to ride. Roughly at that age, the village
would celebrate by giving him his first pair of Cossack baggy
pants ("sharovary"). From spring to fall, boys would spend time
with their grandfathers as a rule, either in the field or with the
flocks and horses. There they would also learn how to fight and
wage war. By age fourteen, a Cossack boy had to be able to
knock a flying bird down with a stone.

The worst dishonor was to be illiterate, and the entire village
would boast of a child who learned in school. If there was no
opportunity to study in school, children studied at home. For
example, Yakov Baklanov, the celebrated hero of the wars in the
Caucasus, learned from his father during a campaign to Crimea.

By age seven, he was as well-educated as schoolboys, and he even knew Moldavian and Turkish. After he returned from the campaign, the neighborhood boys brought him a book. Seeing how well he could read, they included him in their circle. If he had not been able to read, they probably would have beaten him up.

Girls were raised differently. Girl babies were traditionally washed for the first time by the entire female side of the family. It was called "washing away her cares," so that she would have a happy life. The father then had to eat over-salted porridge, and he could not so much as make a face. The first steps of a girl were especially celebrated and gifts were given on the occasion. From age five, a girl was taught how to help raise her brothers and sisters.

For a Cossack girl, it was especially important to sing and dance beautifully. Girls were not taught how to do this, but they were allowed in childhood to dance and sing along with the adults during holidays. When it came time to start a family, the grandfather would give a girl a silver ring, thereby making it known that his granddaughter was "no longer a child."

In the Don, no one would ever dream of forcing a girl to marry. Usually, a young Cossack would come to visit the house of a girl he favored. If he liked her, he would place his cap on the table with its bill facing downward. Now everything depended on the girl. She could take the cap and hang it on a peg, thereby letting him know that he would never be her husband. But if she turned the cap over, that meant that the matchmakers could be summoned.

With such rich family traditions, it's no surprise that even the French wanted to be part of the culture of the Cossacks.

THE HEART AND SOUL OF
RUSSIA'S GREATEST AUTHOR

U p this this point, most of the stories I've shared have to do with war and with the ruling class. But some of the great heroes of history, whose lives really are more interesting than most novels, live what might seem to be simple lives. Only a deeper examination reveals them to be true heroes and heroines, capable of great deeds. One such woman is Anna Dostoyevsky, a person who truly made the career and brilliance of the greatest novelist in Russia's history (and maybe the world's).

"HAPPINESS HAS NOT YET HAPPENED. I AM STILL WAITING."

At the beginning of the twentieth century, recalling his meeting with Dostoyevsky's widow Anna, the Russian actor Leonid Leonidov (he played Dmitry Karamazov in the production of *The Brothers Karamazov* in 1910 at the Moscow Art Theater) wrote the following:

> "I saw and heard 'something', something unlike anything else. But through that 'something,'

through this ten-minute meeting, through his widow, I felt Dostoevsky... A hundred books about Dostoevsky could never have given me as much as this meeting!"

Dostoyevsky always admitted that their "souls grew together." But at the same time, he said that the age inequality—there was almost a quarter century of difference between them—and the inequality of their life experience could have led to a very different result:

 Either, after suffering together for several years, we will part ways, or we will live happily for the rest of our lives."

Judging by the fact that Dostoyevsky wrote this in his diary in his 12th year of marriage, with astonishment and admiration that he was still madly in love with his Anna, their life did indeed turn out to be very happy.

But it was never easy, even from the very beginning. The marriage of Anna and Fyodor passed the tests of poverty, illness, and infant death. It didn't help that all of Dostoevsky's relatives were against the marriage.

Perhaps what helped them hold on to each other throughout all trials was, among other things, the fact that the couple "looked in the same direction." After all, they had been brought up with the same faith and outlook on life.

SIMILARITIES IN EARLY LIFE

Anna Dostoyevskaya was born on August 30, 1846, in the family of an inconsequential official named Grigory Ivanovich Snitkin. Grigory Ivanovich and his family, along with his elderly mother and four brothers (one of whom was also married and had children) lived in a large apartment of 11 rooms.

Anna often recalled that a friendly atmosphere always reigned in their large family. In it, there was no room for quarreling or airing of grievances among the relatives. And so Anna assumed all families were like this.

Her mother (Anna Nikolaevna Snitkina Miltopeus) was a Swede of Finnish origin and a Lutheran by faith. When she met her future husband, she was faced with a difficult choice: either marry the one she loved or remain loyal to the Lutheran faith. She prayed incessantly for guidance in resolving this dilemma.

One day, she saw a dream. In it, she saw herself entering an Orthodox church, kneeling in front of the holy shroud and praying there. Anna Nikolaevna took this as a sign and agreed to accept Orthodoxy.

Imagine her surprise when she came into St. Simeon's Church on Mokhovaya Street to perform the anointing ceremony and saw the same shroud. It was an exact replica of what she had seen and felt in her dream...

From that moment on, Anna Nikolaevna Snitkina lived an intense spiritual life in the church, confessing and communing often. From a young age, her daughter Netochka (Anna, Dostoevsky's future wife) had a spiritual father named Father Philip Speransky.

When Anna was a girl of 13 years old, during a vacation in Pskov, she decided to leave the world and go into a monastery. Her parents managed to get her back to St. Petersburg, but they had to trick her by lying that her father was gravely ill.

Meanwhile, in the Dostoevsky family, "the Gospel was known almost from earliest childhood."

His father, Mikhail Andreevich, was a doctor in the Mariinsky Hospital for the Poor, so the fates of those whom the writer would later make the heroes of his famous novels unfolded before his eyes. The young Dostoevsky learned compassion from his earliest years, both from his environment and his father, even though the latter was a complicated character with a fiery temperament, an odd mix of generosity and gloominess.

Dostoevsky's mother, Maria Feodorovna, whom he loved and respected immeasurably, was a woman of rare kindness and sensitivity. He considered her to be basically a saint. Right before her death, she suddenly came "into perfect consciousness, demanded an icon of the Savior, and first blessed all her loved ones, giving them barely audible blessings and instructions."

It was that same kind, sensitive, compassionate heart that Dostoevsky recognized in Anna Snitkina... He felt: "with me, she can be happy." The emphasis is telling: she can be happy, not I.

Did Dostoyevsky not think about his own happiness? Of course, like any other man, he did. He spoke to his friends, voicing a hope that after all the hardships of a difficult youth, he would finally find some peace. Even as an "old man," he still had hope that he could find happiness in building his own family.

"Happiness has not yet happened. I am still waiting," he said, a person who had already tired of life.

"IT IS SO GOOD THAT YOU ARE NOT A MAN"

As it so often happens, the moment of the decisive meeting came at an unexpected time, a time of tragic, crucial events in the fates of both people concerned.

In the spring of 1866, after a long illness, Anna's father died. His sickness forced Anna to quit her studies in the Pedagogical Gymnasium, so that she could spend more time with her father as he died.

In the beginning of 1866, a course in stenography was offered in St. Petersburg. It was an opportunity for Anna both to study and to care for her father. In fact, he insisted she take the courses. However, after 5-6 lectures she came home in despair: the unintelligible language of stenography didn't come easily to her. Grigory Ivanovich was indignant at his daughter's lack of patience and perseverance and forced her to give him her word the she would finish the courses.

If only he knew how fateful this promise would be!

What was happening at that time in Dostoyevsky's life? By that time, he was already quite famous. The Snitkin family had read all of his works. His first short novel, Poor People, which had been written in 1845, inspired enthusiastic praise from contemporary critics.

But the flattery was quickly succeeded by an avalanche of criticism. His subsequent works met with virulent reviews.

One after another, Dostoyevsky was dealt a series of severe blows. First was his exile and penal servitude, then the death of his first wife from tuberculosis. Finally, there came the sudden death of his beloved brother, an entrepreneur whose many debts Feodor Mikhailovich took upon himself to repay.

By the time Dostoyevsky met Anna, he was financially supporting his 21-year-old stepson (his first wife's son). He was also the financial provider for his deceased brother Mikhail's family. As if that weren't enough, he constantly provided his younger brother, Nikolai, with material help... Later, Dostoyevsky confessed that he "lived all his life in the grip of debt."

By the end of the summer of 1866, Dostoyevsky's circumstances were so desperate that the literary genius was forced to sign an unfavorable contract with his unscrupulous publisher, Stellovsky. Stellovsky, a cunning and enterprising man, promised to publish the complete collection of Fyodor Mikhailovich's works for 3,000 rubles.

However, Stellovsky would only do this if Dostoyevsky completed a full-fledged novel by November 1, 1866. If Dostoyevsky was late even by one month, he would be obligated to pay an inordinate 'penalty'. However, if Dostoyevsky failed to complete and hand over a polished novel before December 1, then all rights to his works would pass to Stellovsky for 9 years.

In other words, Dostoyevsky would have been doomed to

debtors prison and poverty. As Anna wrote in her memoirs, Stellovsky was an expert at "lying in wait until people hit hard times and then trapping them in his net."

The very thought of having to produce a brand new, full-fledged novel in such an impossible time constraint struck Fyodor Mikhailovich with dread and despair.

After all, he hadn't even finished working on *Crime and Punishment*! The first parts of that novel were already in print, so he was obligated to complete it in the near future as well. At the same time, if he didn't fulfill Stellovsky's conditions, Dostoyevsky risked losing everything

And as time passed mercilessly, the prospect of complete failure and destruction became much more tangible and real to Dostoyevsky than the possibility of putting a ready novel down on the table of the exacting publisher.

As Dostoyevsky would later say, Anna became the first person to help him not only in word, but in deed. His friends and relatives sighed and sighed, lamented and sympathized, gave advice generously; however, not one of them actively entered into his practically hopeless situation.

Except, that is, a girl, a recent graduate of a stenography school with virtually no work experience, who one day appeared at the doorway of his apartment.

She, the best student of her graduating class, had been recommended to him by Olhin, the founder of the courses.

"It's good that you are not a man," Dostoyevsky told her after their first brief interaction and the first trial run.

"Why?"

"Because a man would probably start drinking. You won't, will you?"

SO KIND AND SO UNHAPPY

In fact, Anna's first impression of Dostoyevsky was not exactly pleasant.

At first, when the stenography professor Olkhin offered her a job with the famous Dostoyevsky, she couldn't believe her luck. The same Dostoyevsky who was so admired at home! She didn't sleep a wink the night before, repeating the names of the heroes of his works over and over again. She was so afraid to forget, for he would be sure to test her, she thought.She hurried over to Stolyarny Lane with a racing heart, afraid to be late even by a minute, but there...

There, she was met by a man who was tired of life, sickly in appearance, gloomy, absent-minded, and irritable. At times he couldn't remember her name. Or he would dictate a few lines in a row so quickly that she couldn't keep up. Then, he would grumble that nothing good would come of this venture.

At the same time, Dostoyevsky endeared himself to Anna Grigorievna, because underneath it all she could see his sincerity, openness, and trustworthiness. At that first meeting, he told her about what was perhaps the most incredible episode of his entire life, one that he later described in detail in *The Idiot*.

This was, of course, the moment when Dostoyevsky was brought to the place of sentencing for his interactions with a political society with revolutionary ideas. He had been sentenced to death and was already brought to the firing squad.

"I remember," he said "standing on the Semenov square among the rest of my convicted friends. Seeing all the preparations, knowing that I had only 5 minutes to live. But those minutes seemed to me years, even decades...I had so much time left to live, it seemed! We were already dressed in death shirts and separated into groups of three. I was the eighth, standing in the third row. The first three people had already been tied to the posts. In two-three minutes, both those rows would be shot, and then it would be my turn.

"How I longed to live, O Lord my God! How dear life seemed to me, how much good, how much kindness I could have still done! I recollected all of my past, how I had used far from all of it for good, and how I wished to try it all again and live for a long, long time... Suddenly, I heard that we were pardoned, and I cheered. My friends were untied, brought back, and the new verdict was read: I was sentenced to four years of hard labor. I do not remember a happier day! I walked around my prison cell in the Alekseevsky; Ravelin and I kept singing, singing loudly. I was so glad to have the life that had been granted to me again!"

Anna left the apartment of the famous writer with a heavy feeling. But it was the weight of compassion, not disappointment.

For the first time in my life," she would write later, "I saw a person who was intelligent, kind, but unhappy and abandoned by all..."

And as sullen, antisocial, and dissatisfied as Dostoyevsky seemed on the surface, Anna's sensitive heart penetrated through the exterior and saw the depth of his personality.

Later Dostoyevsky would write to his wife:

You usually see me, Anya, as morose, cloudy and capricious; it's just outside; this is how I have always been, broken and ruined by fate; inside I am different, believe me, believe me!"

Anya not only believed but was surprised that anyone could see her husband as melancholy. How could they, when he was "kind, generous, unselfish, delicate, compassionate, like no one else!"

TWENTY-SIX DAYS

The future spouses were faced with twenty-six days of intense work on the novel *The Gambler*. It was in this particular novel that Dostoyevsky described his personal passion for roulette as well as his youthful, painful passion for a very real person: Apollinaria Suslova, an "infernal woman" as the writer himself described her.

Anna typed up the novel in shorthand. Later, at home, often during the nights, she rewrote it into longhand and brought it back to Fyodor Mikhailovich's house. Slowly he himself began to regain hope that everything would work out.

By October 30, 1866, the manuscript was ready.

However, when the writer came to bring the ready-made novel to the publisher, he was told that the latter had left for country and that the time of his return was unknown! Meanwhile, the secretary refused to accept the manuscript in his absence. The head of the publishing office also refused to receive the manuscript.

It was a dirty trick, but one that could have been expected. With her characteristic energy, Anna Grigoryevna entered the scene. She asked her mother to consult a lawyer, who suggested that Dostoyevsky take his work to the notary to document its timely completion. But when Fyodor Mikhailovich arrived at the notary... it was too late! Nevertheless, someone still notarized his manuscript and it was signed by the department of the section. Dostoyevsky was saved from ruin.

(It should be mentioned that Stellovsky, whose name was associated with scandals and underhanded maneuvers in the fates of many writers and musicians, met a sad end. He died in a psychiatric ward before the age of 50.)

And so, *The Gambler* was done. A stone had rolled off Dostoyevsky's shoulders, but he realized that he couldn't part with his young helper. After a short interval, he offered that she continue working with him to finish *Crime and Punishment*.

Meanwhile, Anya noticed a change within herself as well. All her thoughts were about Dostoyevsky and her previous interests, friends and entertainments, suddenly lost their charm. All she wanted was to be near him. Their mutual understanding and proposal took place in an unusual way. Fyodor Mikhailovich started telling her the story of a hypothetical novel. In it, an elderly, visionary artist falls in love with a young girl ...

Imagine, just for a moment, that you are in her place," he said in a trembling voice. "Imagine that the artist is me, that I have confessed my love to you and asked you to be my wife. Tell me, what would you have answered?"

"I would tell you that I love you and will love you for as long as I live!"

On February 15, 1867, Anna Grigorevna Snitkina and Fyodor Mikhailovich Dostoyevsky were married. She was 20, he was 45.

"God gave her to me" – the writer would say about his second wife, again and again.

But for her, this first year of marriage was a year both of happiness and painful disillusionment. She entered the house of the famous writer, the masterful "reader of hearts". She was in awe of him, sometimes excessively, even referring to him as her idol. But the reality of life unceremoniously pulled her down from her elated expectations to hard reality ...

THE FIRST DIFFICULTIES

"She loved me immeasurably, I too loved her without measure, but we did not live happily with her..." Dostoyevsky said of his first marriage with Maria Isaeva.

Indeed, the writer's first marriage, which lasted 7 years, was unhappy practically from the start. He and his wife, who had a very strange character, did not even really live together. So how did Anna manage to make Dostoyevsky happy? After the death of her husband, in a conversation with Leo Tolstoy, she said (though she was speaking of her husband, not herself): "The character of a person is expressed nowhere as it is in everyday life, in one's family."

It was here, in the family, in the mundane life at home that her kind, wise heart was truly felt. From a carefree and peaceful home environment, Anna Snitkina, now Dostoyevskaya, entered a household where she was forced to live under the same roof with the erratic, dishonest, and pampered stepchild of Fyodor Mikhailovich.

The 21-year-old Paul constantly complained to his stepfather about her. When he was alone with her, he did his best to offend her as painfully as possible. He reproached her, for example, with her supposed inability to conduct business and told her that she was causing unnecessary stress for his father, who was already ill. Of course, this was also supplemented by his constant demands for money.

"This stepson of mine," confessed Fyodor Mikhailovich, "is a kind, honest boy; but, unhappily, has a surprising character. He seems to have given himself an oath from childhood, that he would do nothing, have no fortune, and yet retain at the same time the most ridiculous notions about life."

The rest of Dostoyevsky's relatives were also dismissive of Anna. It wasn't long before she noticed that as soon as Fyodor Mikhailovich received a monetary advance for a new book, the widow of his brother Michael, Emilia, or his younger, unemployed brother Nicholas, would appear out of nowhere. Or Paul would suddenly have an "urgent" need. For example, the need to buy a new coat instead of the old one, which had gone out of fashion.

Once during the winter, Dostoyevsky came home without his fur coat. He pawned it to give Emilia 50 rubles, which she urgently needed... The relatives manipulated Dostoyevsky, taking advantage of his kindness and inability to turn someone down. Things vanished from the house. A Chinese vase gifted to them by friends, then a fur coat, then silver appliances...everything had to be pawned.

And so, Anna Grigorevna was forced to live a life of constant debt. But she accepted this calmly and courageously. Another difficult trial was the writer's epilepsy. Dostoyevskaya knew about it from the first day of their acquaintance, but she had hoped that Feodor Mikhailovich's health would improve after the joyful change that took place in his life.

The first attack happened when the young couple were visiting friends:

Feodor Mikhailovich was extremely lively and telling my sister about something interesting. Suddenly he cut off his speech in mid-sentence, turned pale, rose from the sofa and began to bend over towards me. I looked with amazement at his altered face. But suddenly there came a terrible, inhuman scream, or rather a cry, and Feodor Mikhailovich began to fall forward.

After that, I heard this "inhuman" cry, common to epileptics at the beginning of an attack, dozens of times. And this scream always shook me and frightened me.

It was only then that I realized for the first time what a terrible illness Feodor Mikhailovich suffered from. Hearing him scream and groan nonstop for hours, seeing his face distorted by suffering, a face completely unlike his face, his insane immobile eyes, realizing that I completely didn't understand his incoherent speech, I was almost sure that my dear, beloved husband was going crazy, and what horror that thought struck in me!"

She had hoped that after the marriage his attacks would become less frequent. But they continued. She had hoped that at least during the honeymoon there would be time to be alone, to talk and to enjoy each other's company, but all her free time was occupied by guests and Dostoyevsky's relatives, whom she had to entertain endlessly. The writer himself was constantly busy.

The young wife longed for her former quiet life, where there was no room for problems, melancholy, and constant clashes. She missed the short interval between the engagement and the wedding, when she and Dostoyevsky spent the evenings together, waiting for the fulfillment of their happiness ... But that turned out to be so long in coming.

"Why does he, the 'reader of hearts' not see how hard this life is for me?" She asked herself. Her thoughts tormented her. Perhaps he had stopped loving her, finally seeing how spiritually and intellectually inferior she was to him (this, of course, was far from the truth). Anna even considered divorce, thinking that if she had ceased to interest her beloved husband, then she could not stay with him—she didn't have enough humility for it. She would have to leave.

Too many hopes for happiness had been given to me in this alliance with Feodor Mikhailovich, and it would be too bitter if this golden dream did not come true! "

One day, after yet another quarrel with Paul, Anna was unable to remain composed. She collapsed, sobbing, unable to calm down, and Fyodor Mikhailovich found her in this state. Finally, all her secret doubts were let out to the surface, and the couple decided to leave. First to Moscow, then abroad. This happened in the spring of 1867.

The Dostoyevskys would return to their homeland only four years later.

SAVING THE MARRIAGE

Although Anna Dostoyevskaya often repeated that she had been only a child when she was married, she adapted to her new position very quickly. She also immediately took upon herself the responsibility of "family treasurer," a role she fulfilled with ability and enthusiasm.

Her main goal was always to provide her husband with a sense of peace and the right environment for creative production. He worked at night. It is important to remember that for Fyodor Mikhailovich, writing was not just a calling, but also his sole means of earning money.

Unlike Tolstoy or Turgenev, he did not possess a family fortune, so he had to write all his works (except his first story) hastily and hurriedly. He was always rushing to fulfill an order on time; otherwise, he and his family would have been left with no material means for survival.

Cleverly and energetically, Anna began to deal with the creditors that hounded Dostoyevsky. She analyzed and re-analyzed debt receipts, shielding her husband from all these worries. She also took a risk: she pawned her small dowry to go abroad and "save our happiness."

She was convinced that only "constant spiritual communication with my husband can allow us to create the strong and united family that we dreamed about."

By the way, it was only by her efforts that the fictitious nature of many of Dostoyevsky's debts became known. For despite his vast life experience, Dostoyevsky was such a trusting, honest, conscientious person and so little adapted to life that he trusted anyone who came to him asking (or demanding) money.

After his brother Mikhail died, people began to appear at Fyodor Mikhailovich's door with demands for money that his brother supposedly owed them. Among them there were many rascals who had decided to cash in on the credulity of the writer. He never demanded any confirmation from anyone, no documents of any sort; he simply believed them.

Anna took it upon herself to deal with these so-called creditors. In her Memoirs, she admits:

 A bitter feeling rises in me when I remember how my personal life was poisoned by these debts of others ... At that time, my entire life was shadowed by unending reflections about where I could get so much money by such a date; where and for how much I could pawn this or that; how I could manage to keep Fyodor from knowing about the visit of a creditor or the mortgage on something. My youth was spent on it, my health suffered and my nerves shattered. "

But she shielded her husband from her own emotions. When she wanted to cry, she went to another room. She tried never to complain, either about her health (rather weak, though nothing compared to his epilepsy) or about her worries, but always tried to encourage him. Dostoyevsky's wife believed that flexibility was an indispensable condition of a happy marriage. She possessed this rare characteristic to the fullest extent.

Even in those moments when he would leave to play roulette and return, having spent all the money that had been saved to buy them food ...

Roulette was a disaster for the family. The great writer was, simply put, sick with it. He had a wild dream of winning enough money to tear his family out of the bondage of debt. This fantasy had complete control over him and alone he could not find the strength to escape its clutches.

Nor would he have, if not for Anna's unprecedented endurance, love and complete lack of self-pity.

It pained me so deeply to me to see how Fyodor Mikhailovich himself suffered," she wrote. "He would come back from the roulette table pale, drawn, barely standing on his feet and ask me for more money (he gave me all the money for safe-keeping). He would leave and return in half an hour even more upset, get more money and so on until he lost everything that we owned."

And what about Anna? She understood that the problem wasn't a lack of will or desire to change, but that this was a real disease, an all-consuming passion. And she never once rebuked him. Nor did she fight with him. In fact, she didn't even try to refuse his requests for money.

Dostoyevsky begged for her forgiveness on his knees, sobbed, promised to give up the fatal passion... and did it again. At such moments, Anna did not keep a strict, meaningful silence. Instead, she tried convince her husband that everything would be all right, that she was happy. She distracted him from his frenzied repentance by going on walks with him or reading newspapers to him. And eventually Dostoyevsky would calm down.

When in 1871 Fyodor Mikhailovich wrote that he was giving up roulette, his wife did not believe it. Miraculously, it was true. One day, he just gave it up.

 Now I'm yours, yours inseparably, all yours. Up until now, I half belonged to this accursed fantasy."

SONECHKA

In countless families, the loss of a child is the rock against which marriages crash. However, this terrible tragedy, experienced twice in the 14 years of their marriage, only brought the family closer together.

The first time they experienced this terrible grief was during the first year of marriage. Sonechka, their first child and daughter, suddenly died of an ordinary cold, having lived only 3 months.

Anna describes her own grief sparingly. With her typical self-lessness and dedication, most of her thoughts were about another: "I was terribly afraid for my poor husband".

Fyodor Mikhailovich, according to her recollections, "Sobbed and cried like a woman, standing before the cold body of his favorite baby, covering her pale face and hands with hot kisses. I never saw such violent despair ever again."

A year later, their second daughter, Lyubov, was born. Anna, who had feared that her husband could never love another child, noticed that the new joy of fatherhood eclipsed all his prior pain. In a letter to a critic, Fyodor Mikhailovich claimed that a happy family life and the birth of children are three-fourths of all the happiness that a person can experience on earth.

In general, Dostoyevsky had a unique connection with children. His wife wrote that he, like no one else, knew how to "enter into a child's worldview," understand the child, and capture his or her attention with conversation. At such moments he himself became like a child.

Fyodor Mikhailovich wrote the novel *The Idiot* while the family was abroad and finished the novel *The Demons* when he returned to his homeland. Living so far away from Russia proved to be difficult for the couple, and in 1871 they returned.

Eight days after their return to St. Petersburg, their son Fyodor was born. In 1875, another son was born in the family. They named him Alyosha, in honor of the righteous Alexey, the holy man of God, a saint Fyodor Mikhailovich particularly revered.

That same year the magazine *Otechestvennye Zapiski (Notes from the Fatherland)* published Dostoyevsky's fourth great novel, *The Adolescent.* But misfortune struck the family again. Their son Alyosha inherited epilepsy from his father, and his first attack, which occurred when the boy was three years old, was fatal... This time the roles of the spouses was reversed. Anna, an unusually strong and resilient woman, was crushed with grief and could not cope with this loss. She lost her energy, her interest in life, and even became distant from her other children, which frightened her husband.

He spoke to her, urging her to submit to the will of God, to live on. It was during this year that the writer traveled to Optina Monastery and met twice with Elder Ambrose. The elder gave Dostoyevsky his blessing and told him the words that the writer would later memorialize through elder Zosima in The Brothers Karamazov:

 It is Rachel of old," said the elder, "weeping for her children, and will not be comforted because they are not. Such is the lot set on earth for you mothers. Be not comforted. Consolation is not what you need. Weep and be not consoled, but weep. Only every time that you weep be sure to remember that your little son is one of the angels of God, that he looks down from there at you and sees you, and rejoices at your tears, and points at them to the Lord God; and a long while yet will you keep that great mother's grief. But it will turn in the end into quiet joy, and your bitter tears will be only tears of tender sorrow that purifies the heart and delivers it from sin. And I shall pray for the peace of your child's soul. What was his name?"

WHAT DID HE SEE IN ME?

Dostoyevsky began *The Brothers Karamazov* (his last and, in the opinion of most critics, his best novel) in the spring of 1878 and finished it in 1880.

He dedicated it to his beloved wife, Anna.

> Anka, my angel, you are my everything, my alpha and omega! Ah, so you also see me in a dream and, 'waking up, yearn because I'm not there.' It's terrible how wonderful this is, and I love it. Long, my angel, long for me in all respects—it means that you love. To me, this is sweeter than honey. I'll come and kiss you endlessly...
>
> But how will I live through this time without you and without the children? It's no joke, an entire 12 days."

These are lines from Dostoyevsky's letters from 1875-1976, when he left for business in Petersburg, while the family stayed at the summer house in Staraya Russa.

His family became a quiet harbor for him, and as he himself admitted, he fell in love with his wife many times anew throughout their life together. Meanwhile, Anna, to the end of her days, genuinely could not understand what Dostoyevsky had found in her:

> All my life I have seen it as somewhat of a mystery, the fact that my good husband not only loved and respected me, as many husbands love and respect their wives, but almost worshiped me, as though I was some kind of special being, created especially for him. And this was true not only of the time immediately following our marriage, but of all the other years until his very death.
>
> For in reality, I was neither particularly beautiful, nor did I not possess talents or an incredible intellect. I had only a secondary school education. And yet, in spite of this, I earned such reverence and almost worship from such an intelligent and talented person."

Although Anna Grigoryevna and Fyodor Mikhailovich were perhaps not the perfect "character match" (a modern obsession), she knew she could always rely on him. Meanwhile, he could always count on her delicacy and care. He trusted her completely, to a degree that sometimes surprised her.

> We didn't copy each or try to remake our characters for the other, nor did our souls get too entangled in each other's psychologies. And so my good husband and I—we both felt that our souls were free ... This approach from both sides was what allowed us to live all fourteen years of our married life."

That's not to say that their married life was idea. Anna had to get used to living in cramped conditions, in constant debt. Neither was the great writer, of course, always an ideal husband.

For example, he had a tendency to be very jealous and would sometimes flare up, causing a scene. Anna wisely avoided situations that could provoke her husband and always tried to alleviate the consequences of his temper.

During editing, he would often lose his temper. He maintained that some writers were so arrogant that they rebelled against even miniscule changes in their works, like the placement of a comma. Irritated, he would compose very sharp letters to his editors.

The next morning, having cooled down, he would be filled with regret and ashamed at his own short temper. In these situations, Dostoevskaya simply would not mail out the letters, waiting until the next morning. When magically "it turned out" that the hasty letter had not yet been sent, Fyodor Mikhailovich was always very happy. He would write a new one, much softer in tone.

Although, for some reason, the couple's religiosity did not prevent them from visiting a fortuneteller once (who, by the way, predicted the death of their son Alyosha), nevertheless the Gospel was a fundamental part of their lives.

Dostoyevskaya often remembered how Fyodor Mikhailovich would put the children to sleep. He would read the prayers "Our Father", "O Theotokos Rejoice" and his favorite – "All my hope I place in thee, Mother of God, keep me under Thy protection " with them...

SUFFER IT TO BE SO

In 1880, Anna Grigorievna became the independent publisher of her husband's works. She founded an enterprise called "The Book Trade of F. M. Dostoyevsky" (exclusively aimed at residents of other cities) that was incredibly successful. The financial situation of the family improved and the Dostoyevsky family finally repaid their debts.

But Fyodor Mikhailovich did not have many days left to live.

In 1880, his novel *The Brothers Karamazov* was published. This, according to his wife, was the last joyful event of his long-suffering life.

On the night of January 26, 1881, blood gushed from the writer's throat. The bleeding recurred during the day, but Fyodor Mikhailovich calmed down his wife and entertained the children so that they would not be frightened. During the doctor's examination, the bleeding was so strong that Dostoyevsky lost consciousness. When he awoke, he asked his wife to invite a priest so that he could have confession and communion.

His confession took a long time. In the morning, a day later, he told his wife: "You know, Anya, I have not slept for about three hours and am still thinking, and only now I realize clearly that I'm going to die today."

He asked her to give him the Gospel, which had been given to him by the wives of the Decembrists during his exile, and he opened it at random:

> But John forbad him, saying, I have need to be baptized of thee, and comest thou to me? And Jesus answering said unto him, suffer it to be so now: for thus it becometh us to fulfill all righteousness. Then he suffered him. (Matthew 3:14)

"Do you hear?" he told his wife. "'Suffer it to be so' means I will die."

Anna Grigorievna recalled:

> I could not keep back my tears. Fyodor Mikhailovich began to comfort me, saying sweet, kind words, thanking me for the happy life he had lived with me. He entrusted the children to me, saying that he trusted in me and hoped that I would always love and cherish them. Then he told

me the words that very few husbands can say to their wives after fourteen years of marriage life: "Remember, Anya, I have always passionately loved you and never betrayed you, even in thought!"

A POSTSCRIPT THAT LASTED 37 YEARS

Anna Grigorievna Dostoevskaya devoted the rest of her life to republishing her husband's books. Even her Memoirs were written only for the purpose of shedding light on the writer, whose image was already being distorted by his contemporaries. She was only 34 years old when he died, but there could be no talk of another marriage. "Whom can you marry after Dostoyevsky?" She joked. "Maybe only Tolstoy!"

But in all seriousness, she wrote:

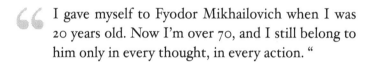 I gave myself to Fyodor Mikhailovich when I was 20 years old. Now I'm over 70, and I still belong to him only in every thought, in every action. "

All her life, Anna Grigorievna collected everything related to Dostoyevsky, and in 1899, she transferred more than 1000 items to the Historical Museum for the creation of a special museum dedicated to her husband. In Staraya Russa, where the Dostoyevsky family often resided in the summer months, she opened a parish school. It was named after Dostoyevsky, served children from poor peasant families, and even had a boarding house.

In the last year of her life, Anna was already seriously ill and experienced starvation in a war-torn Crimea. She died in Yalta on June 22, 1918.

Perhaps someone may be bewildered by Dostoevskaya's self-abnegation and her reverence for her husband, who filled her entire life. But who knows, could it be otherwise? Could anyone less self-sacrificing have endured the trials and burdens that always accompanied Fyodor Mikhailovich? And is it surprising that next to the great writer was a truly great woman?

"Many Russian writers would feel better if they had wives like Dostoyevsky had," said Leo Tolstoy after meeting with her. How did she manage to do it? ... If Anna Grigorievna Dostoyevskaya were asked to give the recipe for a happy marriage with a great writer, it could surely be summed up by her following words:

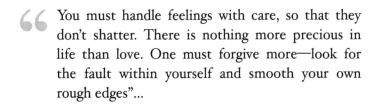 You must handle feelings with care, so that they don't shatter. There is nothing more precious in life than love. One must forgive more—look for the fault within yourself and smooth your own rough edges"...

✢ 12 ✢

THE WAR NO HISTORY BOOK
WILL TELL YOU ABOUT

Perhaps no episode in the nineteenth century sounds more fictional or tragically ridiculous than the so-called "War of the Teetotalers". It *was* a real war, with real artillery barrages, with fatalities and captives, with vanquishers and vanquished, with a judgment over the defeated, with plenty of booty for the victors. The battles of this largely silent war raged all over the twelve regions of the Russian Empire from 1858-1860.

THE 146 WINE MERCHANTS

During this time period, some peasants stopped buying wine and vodka entirely. In fact, entire villages vowed to stop drinking. Why did they do this? Because they didn't want their declining health to line the pockets of the 146 people who were responsible for the sale of alcohol over the entire territory of Russia. Yes, you read that right. There was a cabal of merchants running the alcohol trade in the most powerful empire in the world.

These people were incredibly pushy in their sales. Theirs was such a monopoly that if someone didn't want to drink, he'd still have to pay for the alcohol!

In those years, a very strange practice prevailed in the villages. Every male was assigned to a certain tavern, and if he didn't drink his "quota," or if he didn't pay enough in a given time period, then the owners of the tavern would charge that amount to the local village. If someone didn't want to pay or couldn't pay, he would actually be flogged publicly.

The alcohol sellers, seeing how successful this system was for raising money, kept raising the price of wine and vodka. By 1858, a bucket of bad moonshine (which used to cost three rubles) now cost ten. Finally, the peasants got sick of the system, and they started to boycott the sale of alcohol completely.

IMPROMPTU TEMPERANCE MOVEMENT

This was not so much a decision based on greed or love of money; rather, it was a matter of principle. People could see how the young men in the villages were all becoming alcoholics. Their wives, their children all suffered, and that meant the entire community suffered. As a result, village after village officially announced: "In our village, no one will drink anymore!"

So the wine merchants started by lowering prices. But the peasant's didn't budge. It got so serious that innkeepers started to give out vodka for free, just to put a dent in the new temperance movement. But it didn't work. "We will not drink anymore!" the villagers continued to say.

Here's a concrete example. In the Balashov *uezd* of the Saratov *gubernia* (region), 4,752 people refused to drink in 1858. The village councils put a constant guard on the taverns so that no one would buy wine. If anyone broke and did buy it, they would be subject to fines from the village council or even beatings.

The villagers were joined by city dwellers as well. Workers, civil servants, even nobles joined in. Most importantly, many priests got involved by giving blessings to their parishioners to join the impromptu temperance movement. This is what really scared the wine merchants, and they made an official complaint to the government.

THE OFFICIAL RESPONSE

In March 1858, the Russian Empire's minsters of finance, domestic affairs, and state property issued a series of laws that effectively *prohibited temperance*! The local authorities were told not to allow any local chapters of any temperance movement to form, and any existing village council rulings concerning temperance were declared null and void.

Then, the war began. Beginning in June 1859, in West Russia, peasants began to riot and destroy local taverns. In Vol'sk, three thousand people destroyed all stands selling wine at a local market. In answer, the local police, along with members of the army stationed nearby, tried to calm the rioters. But the peasants managed to disarm both the police and the soldiers. They then proceeded to free all prisoners from their cells. Only after a few days, when the regular army arrived from Saratov, did the riot calm down. Twenty-seven people were arrested.

All of those arrested were convicted based only on the testimony of the wine merchants, who didn't bother to back their testimony with any proof. Interestingly, historians note that there are no official records of anyone stealing money during these riots. Instead, tavern owners stole money from their own taverns, then blamed the loss on the rioters.

During this particular riot, thirty-seven taverns were torn down, and for each one of these the local peasants were heavily fined and forced to pay for the reconstruction. The few soldiers who took the side of the temperance rioters were deprived of their freedom and all honors they may have received. Some were even sent to Siberia.

All over Russia, over 11,000 people were jailed for trying to stop their own people from becoming alcoholics. Riots were everywhere calmed by Imperial armed forces, who were even given the order to shoot to kill. All over the country, violent reprisals took place against those who dared to protest what was effectively an officially-sanctioned "alcoholization" of the populace. Judges gave furious convictions. They were commanded not merely to punish the rioters, but to make examples of them, lest anyone strive to begin any movement of "temperance without official authorization."

That still left the problem of future riots, so the authorities decided to buy the cooperation of the peasants. They instituted an excise tax on alcohol, and basically allowed anyone (not the 146 specially licensed merchants) to sell alcohol as long as they paid the excise tax. After that, they had much fewer problems with temperance activists...

❧ 13 ❧

RUSSIA'S SECRET TSAR

The problem of power and personality is one that has fascinated people from the beginning of history. We are going through our own particular version of it right now in America. Everyone seems to be at war with the President and Congress. Then we have a strange, sometimes morbid, obsession with Vladimir Putin in Russia.

I am fascinated by individuals in history who manage to reach an apex of power where he (or she) directly affect the domestic and foreign policy of entire nations. It's not so much the politics that fascinate me, though. More interesting is the effect of that power on the individual, the interior conflicts and reality of someone who can dispose of the fates of thousands with a wave of his hand. Where does concern for one's country begin and self-interest end? How can the personal strengths and shortcomings of such individuals help or hinder their work? Can their mistakes destroy nations?

As I started to research books 4 and 5 of my epic fantasy series, I read a fascinating character study of a man some people believed to be the real power behind the throne of Alexander III and Nicholas II. A man whose political and personal demise coincided with the demise of one of the greatest empires this world has ever seen.

THE "GREY CARDINAL"

Konstantin Petrovich Pobedonostsev is a significant figure in Russian history and culture. Even so, he remains a bit of a mystery, both to his contemporaries and to us. Many myths have been created around his incredible energy and activity. Some consider that he was the power behind the throne of Alexander III and Nicholas II. Others consider him to be the head of a conservative reactionary movement that championed censorship. Some say outright that he dreamed to plunge the country back into the Middle Ages. The liberal intelligentsia hated him, but plenty of conservatives couldn't stand him either.

Pobedonostsev was born in 1827 in Moscow. His grandfather was a priest, and his father was a professor of literature in Moscow University. In 1846, he finished his study of law at the Imperial College of Law. He prepared for a political career and soon became a senator and a member of the National Council. From 1880, he became the Ober-Procurator of the Most Holy Synod and a member of the Committee of Ministers, one of the highest political positions in the land.

Other than being the political administrator of the Church, he influenced national politics and education policy, as well as international affairs. From 1884, he energetically promoted a national program of parochial schooling for children of all social classes. By the end of the 20th century, nearly half of all children in Russia were taught at such schools. He was also personal friends with Dostoyevsky.

"WITH WINGS LIKE AN OWL"

Most Russian people know Pobedonostsev best from a poem by Alexander Blok:

In those distant, deaf years
Dream and dark ruled over hearts
With owl-like wings, Pobedonostsev
Flew over the skies of Russia.

And there was neither day, nor night,
Only the shadow of those wings.
He drew a magic circle around Russia,
Staring her in the eyes
With a glassy wizard's stare.

AND TO THAT music of the magic story,
The beauty fell asleep with ease,
Enveloped in his magic mist,
And all her thoughts and hopes and passions slept..."

BLOK UNDERSTOOD that Pobedonostsev was something extraordinary. He never met him, but he knew people who had regular meetings with him or even were his friends. We see from the poem that Blok himself doesn't quite know what to make of him.

Pobedonostsev was remarkably unattractive, reminiscent of Koschei the Deathless, a popular figure from fairy tales. But when he started to speak, all such comparisons faded away. He was a fabulous orator, managing to almost hypnotize people by his speech, even if they were his enemies. So this image of the wizard, sometimes frightening, but always intelligent and hypnotic, is not accidental in Blok's poem.

CONSERVATIVE VS LIBERAL

Everything Pobedonostsev did, as indeed everything in Russia at that time, must be measured by the monumental events of the

1860's, in particular the abolishment of serfdom. Culturally and politically speaking, everything in Russia was a response to that event. For example, there was the liberal answer to those early reforms. Liberals clamored for Russia to follow the path of European industrial development. Then there was the revolutionary response that considered all the reforms insufficient. Finally, there was the conservative response.

One of the conservatives was Konstantin Pobedonostsev. He and many others of his ilk considered the liberal and the revolutionary responses as two sides of the same coin. In fact, Pobedonostsev considered the liberals even more dangerous than the revolutionaries, because they paved the path to revolution.

The conservative response was to come up with a complete and very attractive political and cultural program. In part, it was centered on a conception of the so-called "common folk" of Russia and an attempt to save the traditional values that they believed were being preserved in the sphere of the "folk."

However, the "folk" is always a kind of huge, mute animal that no one really understands. What is he thinking, what is she feeling? Everyone had their own ideas, and no one really bothered to ask the folk themselves. The revolutionaries believed the folk to be the natural soil in which the revolution would be cultivated. But the conservatives saw something completely different in the "common man."

Pobedonostsev was effectively cutting the ground from under the revolutionaries' feet when declared that he spoke for the people, not for the narrow-minded elite that was more interested in foreign reforms than the true good of the Russian people. He said that the "common people" were nothing like the revolutionaries imagined. The Russian folk are patriarchal, he said, devoted to the Tsar, monarchist to the core, profoundly religious, seeing no possible life outside the Church.

Pobedonostsev's grand and unprecedented political and cultural program to develop parochial schools came out of such views concerning the nature of the Russian people. As strange as it may sound, it was actually a very democratic project. He tried to give the people the opportunity to take the initiative themselves to create something that both he and they would be proud of.

This was a course of study centered of the study of religious texts first and foremost, of church chant and the Slavonic language. In this case, the school was intimately connected with the Church, and education went hand in hand with active participation in the daily life of the local church. As Pobedonostsev said, "This is what the people want. I am merely expressing their will."

PEOPLE, NOT INSTITUTIONS.

Some people even go so far as to call Pobodonostsev the "ideologue of the reactionary policies of Alexander III," when all the reforms of the 1860's were slowly scaled back. However, nothing could be further from the truth. The conservatism of Alexander III's time had many different aspects. It was not a single, unified political ideology. Pobedonostsev represented only one of these aspects. And he was very skeptical of the reactionary policies designed to scale back the reforms of the 1860's.

This is because he was afraid of any and all kinds of change in the administration and political institutions of Russia. He believed that the 1860's had done enough damage in terms of total societal change. It was better to stay the course than to encourage any more changes, even conservative ones. It's like zugzwang, a stalemate in chess where every move worsens your general situation.

At the same time, he was a proponent of tight control over anything that had to do with information, culture, and education. And his actions were often severe and uncompromising. Hence his popular image as a "dark wizard" or "grey cardinal."

Still, he didn't control the entire apparatus of government, even if he did have influence over the bureaus of censorship, culture, and education. Officially, as Ober-procurator of the Synod, he had limited authority over the politics of censorship, but in fact, he was a kind of tsar in the censorship office, ruling it as he saw fit.

But rather than using this position arbitrarily, Pobedonostsev personally read nearly every single item that was published in official Russian channels. He was an incredibly hardworking man. At that time, if you applied yourself, you could read most of what was published in Russia in any given year. In our own time of the internet, this seems incredible.

As for Pobedonostsev's answer to the eternal question, "What is to be done?", he believed that the answer was to be found by influencing people directly. One of the aspects of his program can be defined thus: "People, not institutions." He believed that everything would get better only if the government took an active interest in forming the inner world of people through social consciousness, schools, and the culture at large.

That's why he was so active in censorship, not because he was interested in suppressing information, but because he was interested in cultivating minds and hearts. Another aspect of this "cultural formation" was his control over the fine arts. His influence could remove famous paintings from official galleries. For example, he had Ilya Repin's famous "Ivan the Terrible and His Son Ivan" removed.

At the same time, he supported many artists personally. He also encouraged many famous composers, especially when they turned to composing church music, including Tchaikovskii himself, for whom he managed to get a personal grant from Alexander III himself.

THE CHURCH AND THE GOVERNMENT

As strange as this may seem, Pobedonostsev was one of the first Ober-procurators (government ministers in charge of the administration of the Russian Church) to actually be a pious Christian. Most of his predecessors failed to even appreciate the significance of the Church for the State. Pobedonostsev, on the contrary, saw the Church as giving a moral foundation to the nation that was indispensable, if the government were to accomplish anything at all.

His view of the government was interesting. He considered government to be part of a larger social organism, and that a large part of government's responsibilities were to take care of the spiritual life of society. He considered that all financial growth, institutional improvement, or political projects were pointless if the spiritual foundation of the society at large has been undermined. And the spiritual foundation of Russia, he believed, was the worldview of the common people, which was founded on the Orthodox faith and Church.

The government, then, should be first of all involved in fulfilling the spiritual requirement of society, even before political ones. Thus, ideological or political goals were subservient to spiritual ones. For example, in the 1860's, part of the reforms called for the closing of a certain number of parishes and priestly positions (which were government positions at the time) in the interest of fiscal economy. Pobedonostsev considered such an idea to be detrimental not so much to the church, as to the government, and he actively campaigned against it.

For him, the most important job of government was to preserve and uphold the traditional, religious worldview of the common people. If the government were to close parishes and churches, then the government would risk an upheaval in the worldview of the folk. If the government is an Orthodox one, it cannot close churches, because if it does, it ceases to be Orthodox, and it breaks its link with the common people. And if the people realize that the government is effectively no longer Orthodox, that, in Pobedonostsev's mind, would lead to revolution.

It may seem strange to a Western mind to consider the

Church being so subservient to the State. However, at that moment in time, giving the Church more independence in the social space was effectively impossible. The Church and State had become so intertwined that any change in their relationship without a complete shift in the style of government was impossible. It is enough to mention that though the country became a constitutional monarchy in 1905, the relationship with the Church didn't change one bit.

REVOLUTION

After the Revolution of 1905, Pobedonostsev famously said, "I did warn you all." However, he was shocked, destroyed, undone by the chaos of that first revolution. He saw no way out of the situation. He was especially shocked when several church hierarchs, including the effective head of the church, Metropolitan Anthony (Vadkovskii) of St. Petersburg, spoke out against him. After all, he had considered that everything he did, he did first of all for the good of the Church.

The irony, of course, was that he never gave the Church any freedom, keeping all authority to himself. He ruled over the Synod of bishops like an autocrat, cutting off any discussions he didn't like even before they started. Naturally, the bishops protested. But rather than listen, he simply instituted even more draconian measures to silence them.

Paradoxically, he wanted the Church to be independent of the government, but only under his patronage and favor. He believed that he was the only person in all of Russia who truly understood the needs of the people and the Church. He thought that he alone knew what needed to be done and what direction was best.

What complicates his persona even more is that he was clearly an ambitious man who wanted power. He hated the direction the country took in the 1860's, taking many of the reforms as a personal offense. He was, it must be said, an expert in

Russian law, but his recommendations for the proper administration of reform in the 1860's were summarily ignored. So his rise to power was at least partially motivated by a desire to show everyone that they had been wrong to underestimate him.

And for all that, he had a creative or even mystical component to his personality. He thought of himself as a kind of prophet, a bearer of the truths of the principles of the common people. And he believed that quiet, efficient local reform would slowly rework the fabric of society to make it eventually a truly "Holy Russia."

In effect, despite his conservatism, Pobedonostsev was a utopian at heart. His worldview was based on a myth, even though it was a beautiful one. This myth was that the common man was at heart religious, patriarchal, and monarchist. Another aspect of the myth was that quiet work on a local level could effect monumental societal change. It was a belief that if only he could influence the spiritual worldview of the people, he could fix all of Russia's social problems.

At the heart of this myth was a belief that there is movement in history, that Russia is somehow equal to itself at all times and will remain the same, in some sense, forever. Because he believed that, he abhorred all change as inherently evil. But to be able to contain Russia in this stasis and yet effect small changes on the level of the human heart—this is the work of a superman. And for all his influence, Pobedonostsev was no superman, and he died a broken and disillusioned man.

✾ 14 ✾

AN ILL-FATED CORONATION

The problem of ideal government has bothered people for millennia. Perhaps until very recently, some people might have considered this problem to be resolved. Some honestly believed in the universal triumph of democracy as the perfect government. However, the current disaster of democracy both in the US and in other places may have shaken the faith of some. Others take heart in the defeats of such anti-establishment types as Marine le Pen, without seriously considering how much her defeat may have to do with the death of democracy and the rise of a new financial oligarchy.

My novels are not political or philosophical tracts. Far from it. But like any conscientious person, the problem of ideal government is one that concerns me as a human being. So naturally some of that spills into my fiction. In particular, my second novel can be read as an exploration of the traditionally Russian idea of "anointed monarchy" (not, I hurry to add, "absolute monarchy").

One of my characters even gets physically anointed in a ceremony that's meant to evoke as much a sense of religious majesty as political triumph.

The inspiration for that scene is the coronation of Nicholas

II. It was a coronation remarkable both for its pomp and its tragedy. On the fourth day of the celebration, there was a mass hysteria in a crowd of 500,000, and almost 1,500 people were trampled to death. The responsibility for this tragedy on the "Khodynka" is one of the many accusations flung at "Bloody Nicholas" by shoddy historians.

The reality of the coronation, anointing, and subsequent tragedy is much more nuanced.

THE TSAR'S ARRIVAL

The Tsar arrived in Moscow on his birthday, May 6 (Old Calendar). Three days later, he triumphantly rode into the center of the city. On May 14, (May 26 by our reckoning) the Tsar and Tsaritsa approached the Cathedral of the Dormition in the Kremlin. The Metropolitan of Moscow blessed them before they entered. He spoke to them in a traditional exhortation, rather than a simple greeting. Here are some of his words:

 You are entering this ancient holy place to crown yourself and accept holy chrismation...All Christians receive this sacrament, and it by nature cannot be repeated. If you must accept the imprint of this mystery a second time, then the reason is as follows. There is no more difficult or exalted power than a Tsar's power. There is no heavier burden than the service of a Tsar. Through the visible sign, you receive invisible power, acting from Above. May it illumine your autocratic rule to the good and to the joy of your faithful subjects."

THE CORONATION

All the hymns of the coronation were, of course, symbolic. For example, the Royal entrance was accompanied by the singing of Psalm 100:

> I have set no unlawful thing before mine eyes...A froward heart hath not cleaved unto me; I did not know the crafty man that turned away from me."

The reading from the Old Testament was from Isaiah:
Behold, I painted your walls on My hands, and you are continually before Me."
The Gospel reading was about, fittingly, rendering to Caesar the things that are Caesar's.
The coronation prayer, uttered by the Tsar himself, is particularly interesting:

> You, my Master and Lord, instruct me in every deed that You lay before me. Make me wise and direct me in this great service. Let the Wisdom that sits at the right hand of Your throne be with me. Let my heart be in Your hand, that I may turn everything to the benefit of the people You have given me, and to Your glory."

What is especially notable about these and all the speeches and prayers on Coronation day is how little they flatter the person of the monarch. They are serious, full of warning, and constantly directed toward divine help for this most difficult of vocations.

ANOINTING

The actual anointing occurred after the coronation, at the liturgy when both Tsar and Tsaritsa received Holy Communion. According to the historian Uspenskii, the repetition of an unrepeatable sacrament gave the Russian Tsar a special status. He was now on a kind of separate sphere of existence. His political power had effectively transformed into charismatic power.

According to Fr. Maxim Kozlov, a professor at the Moscow Theological Academy:

> The meaning of this sacrament is that the Tsar was blessed by God not only as the head of state, but as a bearer of theocratic service, which is an ecclesiastical service, as we see in the Old Testament. He is a kind of representative of God on earth." (link to Russian article)

Later in the same article, Fr. Maxim reminds his readers of Metropolitan Philaret's teaching concerning monarchical power: "The people that respect their Tsar please God, for the kingship is a divine institution." (This is another reference to the anointing of Saul in 1 Samuel)

AFTER THE CORONATION

From the early morning of May 18 (May 30 by our reckoning), a huge crowd gathered in the Khodynka Field. There were more than half a million waiting for the traditional gifts given by the newly-crowned Tsar. The gifts included:

- A painted aluminum cup with the monogram of the new Tsar and Tsaritsa
- Half a pound of sausage

- A rolled fruitcake
- A specially stamped cake
- A bag of sweets and nuts

Everything was calm until six in the morning. Then, a rumor started to circulate: There were not enough gifts to go around, and the stewards of the feast were hoarding it up for themselves. Then, as an eyewitness recalled it:

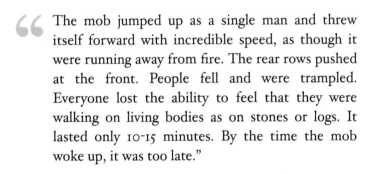

> The mob jumped up as a single man and threw itself forward with incredible speed, as though it were running away from fire. The rear rows pushed at the front. People fell and were trampled. Everyone lost the ability to feel that they were walking on living bodies as on stones or logs. It lasted only 10-15 minutes. By the time the mob woke up, it was too late."

THE VICTIMS OF THE "KHODYNKA"

In the "canonical" list of accusations against Nicholas II, this tragedy is not quite at the top, but still has an important place. He is accused of heartlessness, because he decided not to refuse the invitation of the French ambassador to a ball. The problem is one of a lack of understanding of the rules governing behavior in the 19th century. The ambassador of France was, for all intents and purposes, of equal importance with the ruler of France. To refuse him would be to offend the French government, which, in the pre-WWI, nationalistic age of the late 19th century, was not merely rude, it was dangerous.

Here is the full truth of that terrible day. All triumphal events were canceled from that moment. As for the "heartless" Tsar, he personally gave 1000 rubles to every victim's family. (This is a huge sum of money by our standards.) Together with his wife, he visited the hospitals that held the wounded victims of the catastrophe. The widowed empress, Nicholas's mother, was there as well, and she had this to say:

 I was very upset seeing all these innocent victims. Nearly every one of them lost someone dear to them. But at the same time, they were so significant and noble in their simplicity, that they all tried to get up and stand on their knees before the Tsar! They were so touching, not blaming anyone other than themselves. They even asked forgiveness for distressing the Tsar! You could be proud in the knowledge that you belonged to such a great and wonderful nation. Other social classes should have taken their example, not started to eat each other..."

It's a fascinating eye-witness account. Unfortunately, the "eating of each other" only continued until the age-long love of the people for their Tsar, so vivid in this episode and in the story I share in the next chapter, completely disappeared. In its place came the desire for "the right to dishonor," as Dostoyevsky put it.

❧ 15 ❧

A TALE OF THE TSAR AND A
SABLE

About seven years ago, my dear wife—then my fiancée—and I were preparing for the worst of all fates—a four-month-long separation preceding our wedding. I saw her off at the airport (JFK, I think). It was all appropriately teary-eyed and quite pathetic (in the best sense, of course). As I watched her turn the corner past the Massive Machines of Useless Privacy Infringement, I wandered forward toward her. There was hardly any line of people, no massive push, everything was peaceful. I think I could even hear birdsong.

Before I knew what had happened, an extremely rude and fat man accosted me, demanding to know if I had a ticket. I looked and saw that my lovelorn legs had carried me past the point of no return. Ticketless, I had somehow managed to get all the way to the security checkpoint.

We all know the drill. I was almost carted off in handcuffs, the man only slightly abashed when he realized that the reason for my great breach of protocol was true love.

We live in a supposedly free society. Any attempt at coercion, and we're up in arms. We bristle at the least mention of words like "obedience," "command," or "duty." And yet, we willingly put up with more and more limitations on said freedoms for the sake of safety or comfort or peace of mind.

It is often said in the history books how Tsarist Russia was a backward and authoritarian state. Secret policing, policies restricting personal freedoms, rigid and stifling bureaucracy. And the history books, so far as facts go, are probably right. But the Russian people had something that we have not had for a very long time. A personal and ardent love for the person of their ruler that excused much in the way of bad policies. And in Tsarist Russia, it was actually possible to walk right up to the gates of the Winter Palace and ask to see the Tsar.

Here is a wonderful little tidbit from the recollections of a civil servant. Little stories like this really make me wonder whether we have it all wrong politically and culturally here in the twenty-first century. And were it not clearly written down in the memoir of a civil servant, I would think it were nothing more than a fairy tale...

FROM THE REMINISCENCES OF A. A. MOSOLOV, THE DIRECTOR OF THE OFFICE OF THE MINISTRY OF THE IMPERIAL COURT OF RUSSIA

I sat in my office, preparing a quick presentation concerning patents to be granted by the court, and ordered that no one be admitted. But an old courier entered anyway, and said, "There is an old man and his wife here. Straight from Siberia. They brought an offering to the Tsar, a living, tame sable. They asked me, quite piteously, to tell you that they have no money for a hotel."

I asked the courier, "You feel sorry for them?"

"Yes, sir."

"Well, send them in then."

In walked a venerable old man with his old woman, very presentable. He told me he was a hunter by trade, and that he had the luck to catch a living sable. He and his wife tamed it, and they wanted to make a gift of him to the Tsar. "It's a rare sable," he said. They gathered all the money they had, which should have been enough for a trip to Petersburg and back.

He showed me the sable, who immediately hopped on my table and began to smell my presentation to the court. The old man whistled in a special way, and the sable immediately jumped back to his arm, climbed up his sleeve to the back of his neck and peeked out at me from there. I asked how they came to my office.

"We had enough money, it turns out, only to reach Moscow. From there, we decided to walk, but some nice *barin* (estate owner or lord)—God give him health!—bought us a ticket to Petersburg. We arrived in the morning and went straight for the Winter Palace. They didn't let me in, but sent me to the captain of the guards. He directed us here. We don't have a penny left, but we so want to see the Tsar."

I decided that a living sable might be very pleasant for the young crown princesses. Only an hour later, I was told that the Empress herself had ordered that both old people be sent to the Winter Palace, and quickly, since the children could hardly wait to see a live sable. I told the same courier to bring them there, and to bring them back to me after the audience.

I waited for a long time. It turned out that they spent more than an hour with the children, and the Tsaritsa was there the entire time. The old man and woman talked a long time about how kind the Empress was to them. He offered to keep the sable until a cage could be got, but the children did not want to lose sight of the animal, and finally the Tsaritsa agreed to let the sable stay. The old Siberian insisted that he had to see the Tsar, and that he could not return to Siberia before he saw him.

On the following day, in the morning, I received an order to send the Siberians directly to the palace around six in the evening. They returned to me after eight. Here is the old man's tale:

"My sable made quite a mess. Broke some things and chewed

some others. When I walked in, he immediately jumped on me and hid behind my collar. The Tsar entered. We fell to his feet. The sable crawled out and also seemed to understand that he was before the Tsar. He stood still and waited. The Tsar took us to the children's room, where I was told to release the sable. The children began to play with him; since we were there, he behaved himself. The Tsar told us to sit and said, 'Well, tell me everything: how you decided to come here, how was your journey, and how you managed to come before the Tsaritsa.'

"I told him, and the Tsar kept asking about Siberia, about the hunting there, about our way of life. Seeing what a mess the sable made, the Tsar decided to give him to the care of the royal hunters at Gatchina.

"I protested, 'Tsar-father, our provider, it would be sad to give him into the hands of a hunter unknown to me personally. One of them will want the pelt and will kill the sable, then say that it died of natural causes. I know these hunters. They do not love animals. Only their pelts.'

"'No, my brother,' said the Tsar, 'I would pick a good one. But perhaps you would be the best keeper. Take him home with you and take care of him well while you live, and you will have fulfilled my command. Look after him, do you hear? He is my sable now. God be with you on your journey!'

On the next day, the Tsar, without waiting to be asked, told the minister that he spent two hours of conversation with two old Siberians and that for him it was a real holiday, so interesting it was for him to know the way of life of Siberian hunters and peasants in general. He ordered that the old man be given a watch with the Imperial coat of arms and the old lady a brooch. He paid them several hundred rubles for the sable and paid for their return journey far in excess of their needs. The old man and women were absolutely thrilled.

Of course, the children were upset, but "Papa said it was for the best."

✺ 16 ✺

WHAT IF THERE HAD BEEN NO REVOLUTION?

W hat might have happened if there had been no revolution in 1917?
The Russian Revolution of 1917 was an event that shook the world, mostly through its aftershocks. We still live in a world that is defined by the changes that occurred during that fateful year. Being a child of the Russian immigration, this event has also always been important for me, though it occurred 100 years ago.

But since this little book revels in that fuzzy line between history and fiction, let's indulge in a bit of fantasy.

What if the Revolution had never happened? Could it have been avoided? At what moment did it become inevitable? What would the world look like now if there were still Tsars in Russia?

A few years ago, the editors of the Russian magazine *Foma* asked several Russian historians their opinion on the subject. Here's what they had to say.

VLADIMIR LAVROR, PROFESSOR OF HISTORY

Two alternatives to 1917

The point of no return for Russia occurred in 1881. On

March 1 of that day, Alexander II signed an order to create two representative assemblies with an advisory capacity for the government. He himself said that this was the first step to a constitutional monarchy.

Of course, it was still far from a constitutional government. But Alexander II took the first step, and he did it intentionally. In other words, it wasn't initially a populist movement that pushed the government to change direction at all. It was a top-down decision, and it was motivated primarily by economics. This was, after all, the Industrial Revolution, with its corresponding democratizing influence. And it was far from the first such reform of Alexander II. Even in 1861, serfdom was abolished, an independent judiciary was established, local government was given more authority, and censorship was relaxed.

However, that very day, Alexander II was assassinated by socialists who wanted to provoke a revolution. And Alexander III, under the influence of his teacher Konstantin Pobedonostsev, never allowed the order of his father to take effect.

Neither Alexander III, nor Nicholas II considered the natural democratization of the Industrial Revolution necessary for Russia. They were both extremely pious men, but they had no intention of allowing democracy to ever spread to Russia, as it was in all other European countries. So the catastrophe of 1917, in some sense, was inevitable for that reason alone.

An alternative to the revolutions of 1917 would have been a bloody suppression of the February Revolution. If that had happened, Russia would have been among the victorious in World War I. It would have received Constantinople, the Bosphorus, and the Dardanelles. Russia's economic growth would have continued (and even in 1914 it was feeding all of Europe). It would have probably become the most powerful country in the world. There would have been no GULAGs, no "Red Terror," no forced collectivization. It's even possible that there would never have been a second world war.

But Nicholas II was no Ivan the Terrible. He would have had

to take person responsibility for the bloody suppression of the revolution. Instead, he sent General Ivanov to take care of it, and he sabotaged the orders of the Tsar. Nicholas II was no tyrant. By his very nature he was marked for a different fate—to become a martyr and holy man.

YAROSLAV LEONTIEV, PROFESSOR OF HISTORY

Changes were inevitable. But which ones?
There are always other alternatives in history. However, after February 10, 1917, there was no turning back. On this day, the chairman of the Duma, Michael Rodzianko, visited Nicholas II at the Imperial Palace for the last time. Here's what he had to say:

"Much is already rotten to the core. A change of the entire system of government is an absolute necessity. The current government keeps increasing the abyss between it and the representatives of the people. The ministers use every opportunity possible to prevent the actual truth from reaching the Tsar..."

Later, he and Nicholas II had this dialogue:

"Your Highness, I am completely sure that this is my last conversation with you."

"Why?"

"I've been speaking with you for an hour and a half, and all I see is that you have been led to a very dangerous path... You want to dissolve the Duma, and so I will no longer be chairman, and will no longer visit you. What's even worse, and I warn you that I am completely sure of this, is that three weeks won't pass before a revolution will explode. Such a revolution that will sweep you away, and you will no longer be Tsar."

"What makes you say this?"

"All the circumstances point to this. You can't joke around with the people's will, with their self-consciousness. But all your ministers mock the people. You can't put all kinds of Rasputins at the head of the cornerstone. You will reap what you sow."

"As God grants."

"God will grant nothing. You and your government have ruined everything. The revolution is inevitable." Michael Rodzianko was no prophet. He simply knew of the existence of plots to overthrow the government. All they needed was for the Tsar to leave the capital. This conversation was probably his way of giving the Tsar a "last chance." Possibly, there was another option, which would have been the reconciliation of the Tsar with the Duma, the release of political prisoners. Possibly, the tension that led to the Revolution could have then been redirected to patriotic fervor.

But Nicholas II could not do this, because he would have had to go against everything he believed in. Therefore, he left the capital on February 22, only days before the street demonstrations began. On February 27, the Tsar received this telegram from Rodzianko:

Situation grave. Anarchy in the capital. Government powerless. Soldiers firing at other soldiers. A person trusted by the country must be given the authority to form a new government. You cannot wait. Any wait is like death. I pray God that the responsibility does not fall on the crown-bearer."

But Nicholas II didn't answer the telegram, considering its contents to be nonsense.

Thus, the death of the monarchy was not inevitable. All that was inevitable was a change in the way government was run. But Nicholas was surrounded by people who wanted him to fail. Historians even think that his telegrams were censored by General Alexeev. As Nicholas himself famously wrote in his diary, "I am surrounded by treachery, cowardice, and falsehood." On the next day after his abdication, he wrote, "I've been reading much about Julius Caesar..."

DIMITRII VOLODIKHIN, PROFESSOR OF HISTORY

There was an alternative

I don't think that the catastrophe of 1917 (by which I mean both revolutions of February and October) was inevitable. More than that, I am completely sure, first of all, that Russia could have had a completely different future, nowhere near as bloody. All it had to do was overcome the crisis of 1917. Second of all, the crisis turned into a catastrophe largely because of external factors, not internal ones.

Yes, Russia at that moment had an extremely corrupt, useless, yet self-assured political elite. It was hard to find in the whole lot of them any energetic person of abilities. Instead, most of them were utopians, lazy "thinkers," political radicals who believed in their own dangerous ideals. I think that if there had been a forceful "cleansing" of the upper echelons of society, initiated by Nicholas II, then the situation could have been mitigated.

There were attempts to do this. However, the reality of a difficult war, as well as the sabotage of Russia's political enemies, hurried the destructive process. The situation became more tenuous, and the mechanisms of government became less capable of dealing with the situation quickly.

However, it would be wrong to blame the monarchy. Nicholas II battled against the rising tide honorably, trying in all possible ways to stop the catastrophe from becoming dangerous. He just ran out of time.

If Russia had managed to win the war faster, with a strengthened monarchy and powerful Church at the head, the economy of the country could have prospered. Such a Russia would have probably prevented the collapse of civilization that led to World War II.

❧ 17 ❧

REFERENCES

Each of the chapters in this book is a partial translation, partial adaptation of an article from the Russian internet. Those interested in proper citation will note that these websites don't always do a good job of referencing their own sources. If anyone of my readers is an expert in Russian history, I'd be very pleased if you were able to provide better/more authoritative sources for the historical facts that I've recounted here.

List of websites:

- Russian Cinderella story: https://cyrillitsa.ru/history/68102-evdokiya-streshneva-istoriya-russkoy-zo.html
- Oleg: https://cyrillitsa.ru/history/68377-chto-sluchilos-s-veshhim-olegom.html
- Olga: http://www.pravoslavie.ru/3481.html
- Alexander the Great: https://cyrillitsa.ru/history/70687-aleksandr-makedonskiy-pochemu-on-byl-p.html
- Ugra: https://cyrillitsa.ru/past/39270-stoyanie-na-ugre-kak-zakonchilos-mongo.html

- Ushkuiniki: https://cyrillitsa.ru/history/100650-ushkuyniki-chto-russkie-piraty-delali-s.html
- The Curse of Dmitry: https://russian7.ru/post/proklyatie-carevicha-dmitriya-kak-na-rus/
- Pozharskii: https://foma.ru/knyaz-dmitriy-pozharskiy.html
- Kulibin: https://foma.ru/7-izobreteniy-ivana-kulibina.html
- French Cossacks: https://cyrillitsa.ru/past/32154-kak-francuzskie-soldaty-stali-kazaka-3.html
- Cossack family values: https://cyrillitsa.ru/past/17958-kossacs.html
- Anna Dostoyevsky: https://foma.ru/byit-dostoevskoy-chto-prostaya-zhenshhina-smogla-sdelat-dlya-geniya.html
- Temperance War: https://zen.yandex.ru/media/id/5cb77bfb2022bb00b251e023/ob-etoi-voine-umalchivaiut-uchebniki-5cc85de5bf32e000b08b8a59
- The Grey Cardinal: https://foma.ru/konstantin-vsemogushhiy.html
- The Ill-Fated Coronation: http://www.taday.ru/text/1070923.html
- What if there had been no revolution in 1917? https://foma.ru/drugoy-1917-y.html

ABOUT THE AUTHOR

Nicholas Kotar is a writer of epic fantasy inspired by Russian fairy tales, a freelance translator from Russian to English, the resident conductor of the men's choir at a Russian monastery in the middle of nowhere, and a semi-professional vocalist. His one great regret in life is that he was not born in the nineteenth century in St. Petersburg, but he is doing everything he can to remedy that error.

Made in the USA
Middletown, DE
18 September 2023

38718008R00073